MW01008807

"This book is practical and down-to-eai ___ vision to introduce the chapters written by the beginning therapists, and questions for discussion at the end of each section. The detailed and open way that therapist experiences are described will be of tremendous help and support for anyone practicing marriage and family therapy, particularly for beginning therapists."

– Linda G. Bell, PhD, professor emerita of psychology and family therapy, University of Houston-Clear Lake

"*Case Studies* is a must-read for supervisors and therapists. The stories shared in this text remind the reader of the vulnerability, growth, and hope that is required when learning to be a therapist. It demonstrates the power that good supervision and self-reflection can have on therapists and their clients. I will be using this book in my courses."

– Jacob B. Priest, PhD, LMFT, assistant professor, Couple and Family Therapy Program, The University of Iowa

"While most case books emphasize 'steps' that can appear deceptively simple, *Case Studies in Couple and Family Therapy* provides an honest and humbling look at the emotional rollercoaster – and magic – we call family therapy training. Written for new therapists and supervisors, this collection demystifies the very personal and vulnerable process of becoming a therapist. It is what has been missing in the clinical training literature."

– Carmen Knudson-Martin, PhD, professor, Marriage, Couple, and Family Therapy, Lewis & Clark College, Portland and co-author, Sociocuturally Attuned Family Therapy: Guidelines for Equitable Theory and Practice

CASE STUDIES IN COUPLE AND FAMILY THERAPY

Case Studies in Couple and Family Therapy is one of the first casebooks to have been written from the perspective of the early career therapist and demonstrates how key issues in therapy occur for both clients and supervisees.

The book brings together chapters from trainee therapists alongside expert commentary from the editors who have extensive experience in supervising new therapists. Covering a range of self-of-the-therapist issues, these case studies navigate the complexities of presenting problems, multiple systems involvement, the complication of past traumas, and working in a medical environment, all of which beginning therapists are often unprepared to face. The editors provide introductions to each case study, as well as clinical suggestions and topics for discussion in supervision.

Foregrounding the issues and challenges of the therapist-in-training, *Case Studies in Couple and Family Therapy* is a valuable resource for developing couple and family therapists, as well as supervisors and educators in the field.

Connie S. Cornwell, MA, LMFT-Supervisor, LPC-Supervisor is a clinical fellow and approved supervisor with the American Association for Marriage and Family Therapy, and member of the American Family Therapy Academy. She is the Senior Supervisor of the Family Studies Center at the University of Texas Southwestern Medical Center, where she trains and supervises interns, psychiatry residents, and medical students.

Sarah B. Woods, PhD, LMFT-Supervisor is an assistant professor and director of Behavioral Health in the Department of Family and Community Medicine at the University of Texas Southwestern Medical Center. She is a families and health researcher, and an AAMFT approved supervisor.

CASE STUDIES IN COUPLE AND FAMILY THERAPY

Through the Lens of Early Career
Professionals

*Edited by Connie S. Cornwell and
Sarah B. Woods*

Routledge
Taylor & Francis Group

NEW YORK AND LONDON

First published 2020
by Routledge
52 Vanderbilt Avenue, New York, NY 10017

and by Routledge
2 Park Square, Milton Park, Abingdon, Oxon, OX14 4RN

Routledge is an imprint of the Taylor & Francis Group, an informa business

© 2020 Taylor & Francis

Library of Congress Cataloging-in-Publication Data
A catalog record for this title has been requested

ISBN: 978-1-138-06340-2 (hbk)
ISBN: 978-1-138-06341-9 (pbk)
ISBN: 978-1-315-16106-8 (ebk)

Typeset in Joanna
by Swales & Willis, Exeter, Devon, UK

Visit the eResources: https://www.routledge.com/9781138063419

To W. Robert Beavers, MD, for his commitment to training people in couples and family therapy, and creating a space for this work to happen. – C.C.

To Charlotte Grace, in celebration of her patience and her wisdom. – S.W.

CONTENTS

Acknowledgments   xii

Contributor Biographies   xv

Introduction to the Book   1

Part I
Into the Lions' Den   **5**

Introduction to Part I   5

1   **Rivers of Grief: The Ripple Effects of Loss and Growth**   13

TARA SIGNS

Supervision Issues by Connie S. Cornwell   13

Rivers of Grief   15

2   **Waylaid Secrets and Well-Intended Protections: The Power**
of Secret-Keeping in Couples Therapy   24

BRON KRONBORG

Supervision Issues by Connie S. Cornwell   24

Waylaid Secrets and Well-Intended Protections   26

Part I Conclusion   39

Part II
Family Therapy and Outside Systems: A Slippery Slope   **41**
Introduction to Part II   41

3   **Systems within Systems: Collaboration and Therapeutic Strategies for Navigating Chaos**   49
LAURIE POOLE

    Supervision Issues by Connie S. Cornwell   49
    Systems within Systems   50

4   **I Have a Voice and You May Not Like It: Courage and Connection in a Psychiatric ER**   60
KAREN KINMAN

    Supervision Issues by Connie S. Cornwell   60
    I Have a Voice and You May Not Like It   61

Part II Conclusion   75

Part III
Meeting Myself in the Room   **77**
Introduction to Part III   77

5   **One Voice Among Many: The Goal of Therapy Belongs to the Clients**   87
MINDY HOWARD

    Supervision Issues by Connie S. Cornwell   87
    One Voice among Many   88

6   **Giving Back: A Therapist's Fears Not Revealed**   100
SHARLA AUSTIN

    Supervision Issues by Connie S. Cornwell   100
    Giving Back   101

7   **Close to Home: Learning to Detach When the Clients Are a Mirror**   113
SHIRLEY SHROPSHIRE

    Supervision Issues by Connie S. Cornwell   113
    Close to Home   115

Part III Conclusion   128

Part IV
Concluding Remarks on Supervision   **131**

References   133

Index   137

ACKNOWLEDGMENTS

We first want to acknowledge and thank our chapter authors, Tara Signs, Bron Kronborg, Laurie Poole, Karen Kinman, Mindy Howard, Sharla Austin, and Shirley Shropshire, for sharing their stories. First, these incredible people shared their work with us as supervisees, and reinforced our belief in the power of this work. Second, they shared their growth with us again, as they processed through these stories; therapy, of a different sort. To these authors – we are endlessly grateful for your openness and vulnerability, which has enriched this casebook.

We also wish to express our gratitude for the clients whose stories are captured in these chapters. Each gave permission to their therapist to share their story, such that future generations of therapists could learn from their experiences. We often remark how incredible it is that clients let us get away with all we do – the enormous work it takes to get to therapy, sharing the pain and trauma that often brings people to therapy, allowing supervisors to come and go and guide their therapists. Clients in this book did all this, and then allowed us to write about it. In the writing and rewriting of our own experiences, they gave us another opportunity to learn from them.

As a special note, we also wish to acknowledge the many layers of work we have done together over the years. Though Connie Cornwell directly supervised each of these chapter authors and the cases described, Sarah Woods provided campus-based supervision for many. During this process, Connie provided the supervision-of-supervision training Sarah needed to become a family therapy supervisor, over the course of two years. Thus, it is from a place of truly experiencing isomorphic overlays that the editors have developed this book. We are truly grateful for the experience of learning together.

Personal Acknowledgments

As a supervisor, I (Connie Cornwell) am standing on the shoulders of my supervisors and passing on their wisdom. I especially want to thank Dr. Linda Bell for teaching me intellectual insight takes you nowhere, unless the emotional insight is present, and validation and support is a must; George Pulliam for clarifying all my models, techniques, and trainings are on the shelf and that I have to know what to remove from the shelf that will most benefit my clients; Dr. Harry Goolishian who taught me to speak to the client's listening; Dr. Paul Dell who taught a seminar on Gregory Bateson and Humberto Maturana, imprinting second-order change into my being. And to all the clients I have ever seen, it is a privilege to have worked with you and to have learned from you. I want to acknowledge Dr. Sarah Woods for her insight and caring in coediting this book, which without her help would not have been accomplished. I am forever in her debt. And finally, I wish to acknowledge my husband, Sydney, who teaches me every day about being a couple.

Each supervisor I (Sarah Woods) have had is a significant part of the therapist I have become. I have been immensely fortunate to have fallen in the lap of incredible systems thinkers, and even more fortunate that they embraced me. The memories of some of my clients have faded, though I would have said it impossible at the time. However, the distinct impressions of my supervisors feel as clear as their first mark. The marriage and family therapy faculty at the University of Rochester influenced my belief in the power of self-of-the-therapist growth, interdisciplinary collaboration, and strengths-based supervision. They also taught me, many times over, the value in prioritizing my own family, and modeled for me strength in being a woman in academia. So, too, did Dr. Susan Snyder, who helped me develop as a prepared and boundaried professional, and Dr. Lenore McWey, whose unending support has had immeasurable influence on my personal and professional lives. I am grateful for these teachers' many gifts. And, I am indebted to Connie, who teaches me about courage and standing in my own power, and without whom I would not be a supervisor. Lastly, I acknowledge my husband, Jesse – my secure base.

CONTRIBUTOR BIOGRAPHIES

Sharla Austin, LMFT-Associate, joined the team at the Family Studies Center at the University of Texas Southwestern Medical Center after graduation, working with families, couples, and individuals. She also formerly worked at UT Southwestern's Neurology Clinic, providing medical family therapy for patients with amyotrophic lateral sclerosis, and their families. Currently, she is transitioning to a private practice that specializes in providing therapy for millennial couples, families, and individuals.

Mindy Howard is a LMFT-Associate working toward advanced certification in Emotionally Focused Therapy in a busy couple therapy practice. In her time away from work, Mindy enjoys volunteering with those in housing transition and spending time with her husband working on their farm. She is a member of the American Family Therapy Academy.

Karen Kinman is now in private practice as an integrative mental health practitioner. She integrates therapeutic touch and hypnosis for healing with clients experiencing pain and chronic illness. She works with clients to achieve deeper connection and balance in mind–body–spirit. She is married and has a cat named Trixie.

Bron Kronborg is currently living in Texas with his husband and their two children. Presently, he is working for a regional crisis agency as a master's-level crisis clinician. He continues to focus on learning more about Emotionally Focused Therapy, and has completed an EFT Externship.

Laurie Poole, LPC is currently in private practice working with couples and individuals. She has pursued advanced training in Emotionally Focused Therapy and believes that self-of-the-therapist is an ongoing process and essential component of her professional development.

Shirley Shropshire is currently a LMFT-Associate in private practice. She provides relational therapy services for couples and families in rural and suburban areas.

Tara Signs, PhD, LMFT is currently Clinic Director and Adjunct Professor in the Marriage and Family Therapy program at Oklahoma Baptist University. She is a member of the American Association of Marriage and Family Therapy, and an AAMFT Approved Supervisor.

INTRODUCTION TO THE BOOK

Becoming a family therapist is hard work. Families and couples can be powerful, and test our commitment and resolve. Meeting an intimidating parent or an obstinate adolescent for the first time can lead to a trainee wondering, *Did I make the right career choice?*, and they may feel relieved when the family cancels or does not show. In this early phase of learning, career competency is always on the line, and the lack of confidence may not be easily hidden. It may be especially difficult to cloak self-doubt, nervousness, or fear from a family (with its multiple observers), as compared to an individual client, where a therapist may have much less to manage.

In contrast, this hard work reaps its rewards. Therapy is an incredibly intimate experience. The impacts of becoming a therapist are tremendous and humbling, and the stories described herein highlight how trainees can be moved, permanently, from their experiences with clients. The privilege and power of serving families, and learning with them, occurs from the beginning. Therapists-in-training need not wait to develop into experts to experience the joy that is this work.

Supervising family therapists is hard work. Supervising family therapy interns can keep a person honest and humble, especially as one remembers early struggles and self-doubts. As a supervisor you learn to hold a space of safety, security, and connection for the beginning therapist to learn and grow. What seems a mistake or failure is always a learning moment, and corrections can always be made. As we work in collaboration with our trainees, and they too with their clients and supervisors, we evolve and learn. Though supervisees may dread specific types of problems, diagnoses, or family members, supervisors hope that it is during this supervision process that the intern meets that which they fear the most, especially while they have the safety net of an experienced supervisor. It is a privilege, and often a delight, to intervene with a supervisee, and watch them turn to do the hard work of trickling this intervention down into their clients' family systems. We learn, over and over, about the awesome responsibility it is to be part of this profession, and can experience profound appreciation for the trust of our supervisees and their clients.

Thus, the primary goal of this book is to bring comfort and encouragement to the couple and family therapist commencing their career. Each chapter is written by a family therapy trainee who selected a case that presented them the opportunity for the most growth, especially in regards to self-of-the-therapist issues. They each reveal their personal struggles, and challenges as new therapists, in the hope of providing solace for future learners that they are not alone in the hard work. Indeed, the clinical outcomes of the cases described are positive, negative, exactly as planned, and some nowhere near what was intended. Instead, we aim to emphasize the growth process of becoming a therapist. The effort of learning this trade is not bound by the walls of the therapy room – instead, it is frequently the work therapists do outside of session, and within supervision, that promotes the evolution of their clinical ability. Our hopes are to normalize, validate, and encourage this work, and to promote approaching vulnerability with the dual aim of self-improvement and skill development.

It is also our hope that this book serves developing supervisors. To this end, we provide supervisory context for each trainee's case – specifying what a supervisor might be considering, what impacts a case may have on the supervision relationship, and normalizing supervisors' self-doubts.

More specifically, each supervisee in this book was directly supervised by the first editor (CC). Connie provides her own reflections prior to each chapter, in sections titled *Supervision Issues*. We have also provided ideas about what to reflect on with trainees, at the conclusion of each part. We believe these thought questions may also be important opportunities for new and senior supervisors to reflect on their own trajectories as family therapy learners, and to consider the uniquely developmental, and uniquely systemic, influences on conducting family therapy supervision.

To meet these aims, we have emphasized three core themes that regularly intersect with family therapists' areas of growth, and may commonly appear in supervision.

In Part I, we emphasize the role of *secrecy* in families. We highlight the toxic nature of secrets, how this is compounded when the content of a secret includes past trauma, and specify how Bowenian, structural, and contextual family therapists may each conceptualize and approach secrecy. Lastly, we emphasize how secrets may intersect powerfully with therapists' personal experiences, replicating relational patterns in isomorphic echoes across the client–family, therapist–client, therapist–family-of-origin, and supervisor–supervisee subsystems.

Part II moves outward, with a focus on *larger systems*. We begin by highlighting narrative and medical family therapy conceptualizations of external systems, power, and collaboration, and provide specific supervisory interventions for extending systemic thinking beyond the clients' relationships. We additionally offer a perspective on the contagious nature of pathologizing, and the importance of enhancing therapy learners' sensitivity to dominant, problem-saturated narratives that may be reinforced by other providers. The two chapters in this part are wonderful complements – while Chapter 3 is written by a therapist working with a divided family encountering protective services and mental health providers in external systems, Chapter 4 is written by an intern reflecting on her experience in an entrenched work environment. Both provide perspectives from second career trainees who face the challenge of using their voices.

Lastly, Part III moves deeper into a focus on *self-of-the-therapist*. Though each chapter and part in this book highlights this theme, and the importance of this work, Part III is designed to delve more specifically into the intentional use of self. We provide a broad overview of this construct, across models, as well as describe the inclusion of self in Aponte's person-of-the-therapist model (Aponte & Winter, 2000), family systems therapy, and experiential approaches. We also discuss therapists' fears of incompetence, and the importance of honoring clients' autonomy through ensuring a focus on clients' own goals, rather than the therapist's agenda.

The aim of this casebook is to promote confidence in the fact that the growth experience of learning family therapy is bumpy. Included in these pages are stories of therapists doing this hard work, and then bravely sharing their vulnerability with you, the reader. Therefore, we also wish to provide a disclaimer about suspending judgment. We encourage you to resist reading these chapters with an eye for what you would do, as the therapist. Our goal is not to provide a primer on therapeutic technique or theoretical advantage. Instead, we encourage you to focus, and refocus, your attention on the therapists' vulnerability, and the results they thus achieve with their clients or in their own growth process. It is a professional pitfall to quickly begin analyzing a case for the pertinent facts that help us to conceptualize and treat. We urge you, instead, to attend to your own internal reactions to these therapists and their cases, and consider what it means for your own growth.

Part I

INTO THE LIONS' DEN

Introduction to Part I

As is often the case with rich family therapy cases, family secrets play a large role in the two cases described in Part I. Though the content of any family's secrets may differ, the two examples described herein reflect how critically important it is to pay attention to the *process* of therapy and the family system, versus the *content* of their traumas. For supervisees new to learning family therapy, this can be an especially challenging lesson. Managing the multiple issues a couple or family is presenting with can become much more challenging when some, or all, of these issues are drenched in secrecy and circle around historical experiences of trauma that are rearing their heads to impact family members in the present.

The Caustic Effects of Secrecy

Family secrets have long been an emphasis of family therapy. Secrets involve the withholding of information, or selective sharing across family members (Bok, 1982). As Karpel (1980) identified, secrets may be individual, wherein one person withholds information from the rest; internal, where at least two family members keep a secret from others; or, shared, which he describes as a secret kept by all family members from the outside world. Secrets may also be shared across generations, damning new branches of the family tree to repeat, unwittingly, the patterns of their past.

The power of secrets is held, in part, in the loyalty that keeping a secret conveys. To share a secret with others is often construed as a betrayal. Power is also conveyed by secret-keepers having an advantage over those on the outside. Secrets can, importantly, be understood by their location – in other words, whether the secret is individual, dyadic, or shared can determine how it affects family members, as it morphs the boundaries between them (Imber-Black, 1998). Further, decisions about the secret (active or passive) can ripple across the family system, creating implicit family rules and roles, as well as additional secrets. Understanding how the power of this boundary impacts and contains families requires a systemic orientation (Grolnick, 1983).

Family secrets often have toxic consequences, despite intentions. They result in deception, rigidity, confusion, a lack of differentiation, imbalance, anxiety, and distress (Karpel, 1980). Further, in therapy, the "unanticipated disclosure" of a family's secret to a therapist draws the clinician into the family in a way that they may be unable to navigate, creating a trap or opportunities for the therapist to deceive other, unknowing family members (Karpel, 1980, p. 5). Disclosure from family member to family member can create anger, hurt, resentment, and uncertainty.

Family Secrets Handled by Family Therapy Models

Bowen Family Systems Therapy

Many, if not all, family therapy models include constructs that importantly intersect with family secrets. For instance, Bowen's family systems therapy approach emphasizes emotional triangles or triangulation, the process whereby a family dyad experiences increased anxiety and thus involves a third family member. The purpose of this process is to stabilize the original two-person relationship by spreading anxiety across all three related and interconnected persons and their relational pathways (Kerr & Bowen, 1988). This occurs regularly with family secrets. For example, two family members who share a secret, but experience increased tension regarding that secret, may experience emotional overheating. The increased tension may therefore induce one secret-keeper to disclose the content of the secret to a third family member or to a person outside the family. This process of shifting the system's anxiety by sharing a secret in a third relationship may increase the likelihood that these three family members are able to then keep the secret, as a triangle is more stable and more able to contain anxiety than a two-person dyad (Kerr & Bowen, 1988).

Structural Family Therapy

Second, Minuchin's structural family therapy model outlines family boundaries, or family rules that specify distance between family members, regulating closeness, hierarchy, and roles. Boundaries are dynamic processes and must be renegotiated at each life stage: with the introduction of children, the arrival of children at school age or adolescence, and with the launching of children and older adulthood (Minuchin & Fishman, 1981). Though, there are between-family differences in whether boundaries are allowed to evolve over the life course, and how this evolution is managed.

Specific to family secrets, therapists practicing a structural approach will evaluate a family's boundaries and identify whether they are weak and diffuse, or rigid. Diffuse boundaries between family members are related to enmeshed family relationships, such that family members lack autonomy, independence, and a clear delineation between them. In enmeshed family systems, family members may feel guilt for not disclosing a secret to others, thus feeling at odds with their experience of interconnectedness and reactivity. Conversely, rigid boundaries between family members are associated with disengagement or independence coupled with isolation. Rigid boundaries may distinctly demarcate the family system from the external world, promoting autonomy, individuality, and emotional disconnection within the family, but prohibiting engagement outside the family. Disengaged families may thus more easily maintain a secret from one another, but even more so from exterior systems. This may be a challenging aspect of working with these families – structural family therapists' goals may include promoting connection and support within the family, but they may also find these families are less willing to openly share with the therapist. Increasing disengaged families' allowances and accommodation for family members to connect with outsiders may enhance the healing process and reciprocally increase affection and closeness within the family.

Contextual Family Therapy

Lastly, Boszormenyi-Nagy's contextual family therapy model emphasizes loyalty and trustworthiness, both critical in understanding the nuance of secrecy. Though therapists who practice this approach are not interested in secrets in and of themselves – instead, contextual therapists evaluate the complex ethical principles underlying secrecy and its reveal. For example, Boszormenyi-Nagy and Krasner (1986) specify consideration of who in the family gains from disclosing (or keeping) a secret, what is gained, and the relative balance of that gain. The authors emphasize "discreet consideration" of these principles, "in the context in which a family's secrets have occurred" (p. 343). Though psychoanalytic in nature, this family therapy model is not interested in the revealing of hidden secrets solely for the purpose of developing insight.

Contextual family therapy's conceptualization of split loyalties, or the process of one family member (typically a child) siding with, or preferring, another family member over a third (typically seen in divorce, as when a child feels obligated to align with one parent), has a high potential to engender family secrets. They may serve as a mediator, busy protecting one parent while serving the other. Boszormenyi-Nagy and Krasner (1986) highlight that this pattern results in the child losing trust (current, and the ability to trust in the future), earning destructive entitlement, and coming to believe the world is "intrinsically exploitative and manipulative" (p. 189). Thus, one of the goals of contextual therapy is preventing parentification and the destructive use of others, especially children, to serve adults' own needs (Boszormenyi-Nagy & Krasner, 1986).

Overall, the goal of each family therapy model is to emphasize the relational process underlying the secret-keeping, rather than the content of the secret itself. Secrets are not problems in and of themselves. They may be a function of privacy, security, or protection. They may also be part of the etiology of a family's symptoms, manifesting as a result of hidden alliances and power imbalances. The goal is to assist clients with creating a safe environment for truth-telling such that disclosing secrets is manageable and meaningful (Imber-Black, 1998).

Self-of-the-Therapist Reactions to Secrets: Intersections and Isomorphisms

Originally a concept from mathematics, isomorphism is the idea that patterns replicate across systems. It was introduced to the field of marriage and family therapy by Liddle and Saba (1983), as a relational reconceptualization of the construct of parallel process (White & Russell, 1997). Isomorphism is systemic in that it emphasizes linked patterns, and redundant structures and forms, across groups. In the practice of family therapy, isomorphism can be used to identify replicating processes within the client, therapist, or supervisor systems (and between these systems), as well as to highlight how these systems are impacted by broadly replicating processes in the field of marriage and family therapy (Weir, 2009). Applied isomorphism indicates that what we feel and how we interact in our therapist–patient relationships is replicated in the supervisor–supervisee relationship. It is also how we bring our own family-of-origin processes, and experiences with trauma and secrets, into the room. Isomorphism is also, often, a sneaky process. The replication of patterns frequently occurs below the threshold of our awareness, insidious in snaking underneath our consciousness, waiting to entrap us in familiar, yet inconspicuous, patterns.

As an example, for new therapists, clients' secrets can be reminders of their own family pain, forcing the therapist to revisit these issues with their own family. The intern facing a client's infidelity for the first time can easily become caught up in taking sides with the injured partner while not understanding how it can be a symptom of the relationship. Or, they may become overwhelmed by a new need to resolve a partner's past trauma, suddenly revealed as a couple begins deeper examination of their emotional connection. A therapist's process of joining a family and working to heal their pain can begin to reflect their own family process.

These reactions and processes may also be isomorphically reflected in the supervisor–supervisee relationship. Supervisors who operate from an expert, or hierarchical, stance may find that their supervisees begin to hide how challenging their work has become, or be unwilling to reflect on the pain they experience while unwinding their clients' secrets. Supervisors who are themselves overwhelmed in their work may begin to overidentify with clients' content, falling in with supervisees to become similarly seduced to ignore process.

However, isomorphism is also a key to unlocking the trickiest relational processes. As we learn to spot stealthy imitations across our relationships, we can use our reactions to clients, and mentors, as diagnostic. *What is how I feel right now telling me? What can I learn about this family from how I am experiencing them? Am I carrying that last client into this next meeting?* Our clients' family structures are highlighted repeatedly in their multiple different interactions – learning to identify the isomorphic replications of families' processes across content can, therefore, assist therapists in identifying and understanding their underlying organization (Minuchin & Fishman, 1981).

Isomorphism can also be an intervention: as we recognize the replicating patterns, and our reactions to them, we can move in further to promote connection. And we can learn to be more forgiving of ourselves: as an example, the learning process of becoming a therapist often mirrors the learning process of becoming a supervisor. This can be seen in new supervisors-in-training who decide in the first few weeks, *This is too hard, I have no idea what I'm doing. Why are they looking at me like I'm an expert?* Thus, new supervisors, recognizing their isomorphic learning process, can access greater empathy for their new supervisees, and enhance how gentle they are with themselves.

Learning to understand and identify isomorphism is one of the most critical pieces of learning to be a family therapist. Feeling scared, overwhelmed, and distracted as a new therapist is common – joining clients in their trauma and secrecy can be like walking into a lion's den full of unknown obstacles and hidden potential. Identifying one's own reactions to witnessing clients' pain, and growth, is critical for managing multiple presenting problems, unpacking private stories, and maintaining leadership in the therapy room. Intersections between clients' experiences and thera-pists' own personal experiences of family secrets is inevitable. Recognizing this shared knowledge can give the therapist a sense of the power of secrecy and how secrets can be barriers in families' lives. Similarly, braving the walk into one's own den of family history can help the therapist to heal – a process that can isomorphically transmit healing back into the client–therapist relationship.

1

RIVERS OF GRIEF
The Ripple Effects of Loss and Growth

Tara Signs

Supervision Issues by Connie S. Cornwell

As a supervisor, I try to support interns in not becoming bogged down in all the clients' content, particularly if it is traumatic. However, difficult content, such as suicide, grief, or betrayal, can be overwhelming. These serious types of presenting problems can carry high drama and intensity, and therefore be seductive and enticing. In other words, extreme content can also have an aura of sensationalism in which the therapist can unwittingly become a voyeur to content, at the detriment of the therapeutic process. At the same time, if there is a secret, such as hidden trauma, it can reinforce and perpetuate how scary the content is, and the therapist may fail to make it part of the therapeutic process. In this case, the couple's content was similar to what the therapist, Tara, had faced in her own family-of-origin, and both families had avoided discussing their losses.

At the time I questioned whether the couple case I assigned to Tara was too close to home for her. *Does she need to forgo this case? Or is this the case she needs now for her own personal growth as a therapist?* For Tara, it was questioning whether she was "good enough to take the case." I had to look at the supervisory relationship I had developed with her and question whether it was secure. Did she see me as trustworthy enough to help her through the process? During supervision, through open and honest communication, it was mutually decided that Tara would take this case with the understanding that a safety net was available – she was free to ask for my direct involvement in any session.

In my experience, it is hard for beginning therapists to trust the therapeutic process as they have not had enough experience with process; therefore, I need to continually reinforce that learning. When a supervisee starts to question the process (e.g., *Is therapy working? Am I doing it right? Is it good to deal with the trauma now? Why are they getting worse?*), it is critical for me to support this questioning and help the therapist trust in the process, even though it can feel like a roller coaster. Tara questioned whether she was the "right fit" for these clients and whether therapy was even working. I encouraged her to weather these experiences for the sake of learning and continued to focus on her strengths, thus supporting her resiliency in the face of insecurity and doubt.

Early in the case, an isomorph became evident: as Tara was fearful and questioned her ability, the couple also questioned her about her maturity and whether she was old enough to be their therapist. Not wanting to be caught in this isomorph, and in trusting my supervisory relationship with Tara, I intentionally focused on her competency, reminding her of previous successes in therapy. An isomorphic process occurred: as I stayed steadfast and encouraged Tara, she felt supported and was able to pass on that support and encouragement to her clients who, in turn, began to stand in their own power.

One of my goals as a supervisor is helping interns appreciate that, within their clients, there is a wholeness, a completeness, even if their presentation suggests otherwise. As clients venture through pain and upset, the therapist must hang on and trust in the process and trust in their clients' innate wholeness and their seeking for healing. This supervisory approach allowed for Tara to begin to trust herself, the therapeutic process, and to see the couple as capable of doing the work. Which, as she reveals here, they were more than able to do.

(A link to the interview with this couple describing their therapy experience is https://www.routledge.com/9781138063419.)

Rivers of Grief

Learning the art of therapy is both exciting and scary. As therapists, we have opportunities to create meaningful and rich experiences; at the same time, we face challenges and difficulties that may foster uncertainty or make us question our capabilities. It is undeniably powerful work as we experience moments in the therapy room that often leave us without words. We learn to join our clients in their journey while simultaneously learning about ourselves.

When I reflect on my learning to be a therapist, I often think of Laurie and Rob. At the time I met this couple, I was working toward my postgraduate licensure hours as a family therapist. This training created rich experiences for me to dig deeper into who I was, not only as a therapist, but as a human being. During my master's training, I was learning the basics of how therapeutic models work, and what would not work for me. But during this postgraduate aspect of my training, I felt more confident. I felt I was really able to work through learning Emotionally Focused Couple Therapy (Johnson, 2005), and evolved from a focus on the breadth of family therapy to the depth. I was growing more, and becoming more of my true self. And, I felt I was able to say that it was "ok" to not always be a great therapist; I was in a process of giving myself permission to be exactly where I was in my development. Thus, Laurie and Rob were a large part of my learning to use my authentic self in the therapy room.

Introductions and Initial Sessions

Laurie and Rob, a couple in their early sixties, had been referred to our family therapy center by a psychiatrist who recommended couples therapy. They had been married for over 37 years and had two children, Brian and Michael. Though Laurie had worked alongside Rob for many years, Laurie's role as a mother and, later, as an advocate for Michael, who was diagnosed as deaf, became her priority.

Our early phase of therapy felt like being in combat. Laurie and Rob navigated life with multiple rigid protective strategies that felt like armor. And, their weapons were loaded; at any moment, they were prepared to fire.

At the time of their intake session, Laurie and Rob identified different reasons for attending therapy. Laurie quickly shared that she had concerns that I was not a good fit for the couple – she was concerned I was not experienced enough and expressed that she and Rob would prefer an older therapist. She also voiced feelings of unhappiness and anger, reporting that their marriage was unsustainable. The couple was arguing and distant, and Laurie was concerned that therapy was their "final shot." Though Rob eventually identified similar concerns, he initially expressed that coming to therapy was only to support Laurie through the process. Their diverging motivations for treatment, and their concerns about my ability to effectively serve them, made for an intense and scary first session. I felt a rush of emotions and panic. *What if Laurie was right?* Here I was – young, unmarried, and an inexperienced therapist – asking this couple, who were my parents' age, to trust me! If I failed, then therapy failed, leaving this relationship to fail. Further, in asking about their family, I learned that the couple's younger son, Michael, had passed away at home ten years prior. There was quite a bit of ambiguity about this loss, and the couple made it clear that they had never talked about what had happened for fear of what they might share. Throughout, I mustered every ounce of courage within me to validate Laurie and Rob and be present.

I left that first session overwhelmed with disappointment, ruminating over what I could have done differently. I wished I was a "better therapist." I had had multiple experiences with clients' voicing their uncertainty about my abilities as a therapist. I would create a therapeutic space that reflected authenticity and presence, and clients' concerns often subsided by the second or third session. My experience with Laurie and Rob, however, was different. Rather than being able to hear potential underlying messages of this couple being fearful therapy might not work, I became convinced that this was a result of my "not knowing enough" as a therapist. I feared that Laurie, in fact, was right, and I was not a good fit.

My immediate reaction was to refer Laurie and Rob to a more "appropriate" therapist, a therapist that could offer a path to healing. It was only after supervision that I was able to move past referring the couple and find meaning in this experience. Through my supervisor's presence and safety, she invited me to explore my own fears of working with Laurie and Rob. Initially, I resisted this exploration. I repeatedly thought to myself, *I don't have any 'fears' of working with them, I just can't.* My supervisor continued to challenge and encourage me; ultimately, she believed in me when I could not. I felt scared and pressured to fix Laurie and Rob's marriage, and I cried as I eventually shared my fear of failing them.

The more I accepted my own fears, the more I trusted myself as a therapist. And this confidence came into the therapy room, creating space for trust to grow in the therapeutic relationship. I walked alongside Laurie in her fear, just as my supervisor had done with me. I validated their fears and met Laurie and Rob exactly where they were. I focused on creating a safe, secure space to foster openness, authenticity, and greater connection. As a result, Laurie and Rob began to open doors that for so long were closed to the pain, sadness, and apprehension that lay deep within them. Our first focus of therapy was their relationship process; this enabled the couple to eventually approach the topic of their son's loss. Being able to walk through the previously locked door of grief then provided the couple the tools to open other doors they'd locked.

Theoretical Conceptualization

It became clear early on for Laurie and Rob that repairing and restoring their relationship would be necessary in order for them to understand and make sense of their grief and the loss of their son. I spent the first few sessions exploring the history of their relationship – how they met, what drew them to one another, who pursued whom first. We spent time exploring their early childhood experiences and important relationships. I have always felt strongly that in order to understand *how* a person loves, we must explore how they *learned* love. For example, exploring Rob's childhood experiences that left him feeling lonely and abandoned gave me insight into his panic and fear of disconnection, thus helping me to empathically attune.

After a few sessions, I had a sense of Laurie and Rob's cycle and their attachment fears and desires. Using Emotionally Focused Couple Therapy as my framework, I conceptualized Laurie and Rob's expressions of anger, criticism, and numbness as a response to past hurts and wounds that left them both feeling alone and scared. I observed their sadness and pain as they were caught in a "push-pull" dance; a classic pursue-withdraw pattern. When Rob experienced relationship distress, he would become overwhelmed with anxiety and move toward Laurie, in hopes of closeness. As he pressed for connection and safety through questioning and attempting to solve any problem quickly, Laurie, over-whelmed with Rob's demands and protest, would respond by with-drawing and pulling away.

Rob would perceive Laurie's retreat as rejection and frequently became critical and verbally attacking. The intensity of his protest would leave Laurie experiencing overwhelming feelings of anxiety and, thus, she would pull away further to protect herself. The more Rob protested, the more Laurie would evade. The more Laurie evaded, the more Rob would protest. This dance they were caught in created more distress and conflict, leaving Rob feeling abandoned and unimportant and Laurie feeling attacked and misunderstood. Both partners were left feeling scared, hurt, and alone. Laurie and Rob were both searching for ways to connect and engage and this circular pattern they were caught in continuously hijacked their opportunities for reaching out and hold-ing on to one another. They were stuck in this rigid tango, spinning around and around, until one of them quit with exhaustion.

Though this pursue-withdraw pattern became deeply entrenched in their relationship for many years, the impact of losing Michael exacerbated the couple's emotional distance. Laurie and Rob disclosed that their son had passed away at home, and though they were unclear how he had died, they explained that they believed he had been playing a sort of choking game that resulted in his accidental death. However, the couple explained that when Michael had died, they had never shared the loss of their son together. Because Rob had been the last in their family to see Michael, Laurie explained that she'd always wanted to ask him, "What did you say to him, to make him want to do this? What happened that morning?" Instead, the couple explained they completed the funeral for their son, and never again discussed his death. In one of our very first sessions, Laurie used a boat metaphor to describe her experience of loss. She described this process as she and her husband being in two separate boats, taking individual trips down the River of Grief, unable to connect to one another as sources of comfort. Instead, they traveled down the river alone and scared.

We began to talk about the cycle they were stuck in, and once they began to recognize the negative cycle as their enemy, rather than one another, Laurie and Rob were able to understand their own roles in this dance and that they both experienced hurt and pain. Initially, they conceptualized successful therapy as just walking through every door that kept the sadness, pain, guilt, and fear locked away. It was not until they began to see their cycle itself as the enemy, rather than one another, that they came to understand the deeper need for emotional connection. Developing trust and safety in their marriage would give them the ability to walk through any door that faced them.

Growth for All Involved

As therapy progressed, I had to slow everything down. Them. Myself. The process. I found myself working harder in sessions, attempting to "force" Laurie and Rob to go deeper into their loneliness and fear, thus going too fast and missing opportunities for connection. I became frustrated with feeling stuck and desperately sought out answers in supervision. I wanted the couple to really *get* it, and felt desperate for them to understand their cycle. I continually got stuck in the content of the sessions, and was unable to get the couple to process more mean-ingfully, with depth. I was unable to figure out what I needed to do differently to move through the impasse. And just as I did in therapy with Laurie and Rob, I worked harder to find solutions to my "stuck-ness," rather than being present with my own experiences and learning process.

My supervisor guided me to explore my inner experiences and how they translated into my work with Laurie and Rob. Digging in to my own fear and loss created space and opportunities for me to emotionally connect with myself, and my own process as a therapist. I began taking risks in supervision and, through this, trust and authenticity in the supervision process was deepened.

I became open to my own experiences with losing my biological father to suicide, and began to explore how this loss was potentially influencing my work with Laurie and Rob. I never shared this part of myself with anyone; I hadn't really thought the loss affected me. Growing up, I always told myself that I could not be sad about this loss; I felt I was too young, and my recollection of this experience, and of him, was scarce. My mother, unintentionally, supported this way of thinking. We never talked about him, his death, or the tragedy our family experienced. It was as if this part of our lives had never happened. When I experienced curiosity – wondering what he was like, if he loved me, and feeling like a part me was missing – I would push back, locking the door to this part of my life securely, in fear of what lay behind. My experience of never sharing this loss with others, nor grieving my father with my family, was parallel to Laurie and Rob's experience of traveling down the River of Grief alone. I could not go further with Laurie and Rob, could not explore their vulnerability, as I had not been able to go there myself.

As I grew in my ability to be present with my own hurt, and not be overwhelmed by my emotions, I was more able to create a space for greater understanding between Laurie and Rob. Just as I took risks and began to be open about my loss and my experiences with my father in supervision, Laurie and Rob were able to turn to one another, with trust, and share their deepest fears, needs, and desires. We were able to go deeper into the pain that had kept them from being connected. Rob's criticism and anger unfolded into a fear of abandonment and feeling alone. Laurie's need to withdraw unfolded into a feeling of inadequacy and rejection. Laurie was able to emphasize her need to feel understood and not criticized.

With a secure foundation of safety, Laurie and Rob were able to move differently. Their changed dance honored a new tune – it acknowledged their hurt and sadness, while also reinforcing security. The string that once "tethered them together" was now a "giant conduit of potential," according to Laurie. The progress they made in therapy meant the couple was now in the same boat, with purpose and direction.

They were able to recognize their cycle, slow, stop, and revise their interactions, and create connection which meant they had the relational keys to walk through the door they had locked on Michael's death. Their marriage had become a sanctuary and, together in session, Laurie and Rob grieved losing Michael for the first time in ten years. They witnessed one another's pain and walked through the guilt and blame that once had held them hostage in their relationship. For the first time, Laurie was able to ask Rob what he had said to their son on the morning of his death. He was able to describe what that morning had looked like, and Laurie was able to say, "it's not your fault." As Rob heard Laurie turn to him and provide absolution, he felt "a huge stone has been lifted off my heart." He acknowledged guilt and fear that their son's death had been his fault. Their vulnerability led to a path for deeper and more meaningful connection.

This experience was a profound moment for me as a therapist, but also as a human being. There was such power in being in the room with Laurie and Rob. It was powerful to be a witness to their healing and be present with them; invited into their lives very intimately. This couple modeled for me what it looks like to go to a really scary place, a place that has never been talked about, and be vulnerable. They showed me how to trust the process, as they had trust in themselves – in their relationship and as individuals – they had faith that they could do this hard work. They were ready and they could support one another. I had such respect for this couple's risk-taking in therapy; and, just as they started taking risks, I became braver as a therapist. I became more vulnerable, and more comfortable, sitting with this couple, and other clients, in their pain. Laurie and Rob taught me about the art and beauty of therapy. I began to acknowledge that, yes, I am a therapist in the room, but I am also human; not honoring that would have risked the meaningfulness and success of the work.

Witnessing this transformation also helped me to know that I was ready to approach my mother about my father's death. Though I could not trust my mother – I did not know what her response would be – I had learned I could trust myself. And Laurie and Rob had showed me that approaching what we are most afraid of could work out. They demonstrated how incredibly powerful it can be once you are able to bring voice to the fear. I cry, even now, thinking about it – the moment

Laurie and Rob were able to just sit across from each other, face what had happened with their son, and talk about it. To say, "it's not your fault," and hold each other. It was incredible. Thus, for the first time in my life, I asked my mother questions about my father's death. In the process, I felt the power of vulnerability and deepened my bond with my mother. I found meaning and made sense of what I longed for as a child. I was able to take that risk, inspired by my new understanding of the unlocking of loss, the depth of my supervision, and the bravery of Laurie and Rob.

Use of Self and Passing It Forward

I have been told repeatedly by my supervisor that the universe gives us what we need. I never quite made sense of what this meant until my experience with Laurie and Rob. Therapists are trained in such a way – model- and technique-specific – that we sometimes forget about the power of the therapeutic process. It is our clients that truly teach us about being therapists, but more importantly, they teach us about being human. Being a therapist, and walking alongside clients in their journey, is so rewarding. Laurie and Rob were exactly who I needed, at exactly the right place in my life. My work with them motivated me as a therapist – it was a beautiful process and reinforced why I do this work. My hope is that I was able to be who Laurie and Rob needed as well.

Importantly, supervision had created a safe space for me to take risks, personally and professionally, throughout my work with this couple. My supervisor modeled openness, authenticity, and vulnerability within the supervision process and, in turn, created permission for me to explore my own vulnerabilities safely. Her presence and complete use of self in supervision invited me to dig deeper and find meaning and connection within myself. As a result, I discovered so many important lessons that have shaped who I am today. Most importantly, I learned to trust myself and the therapeutic process. There will be times when you begin to doubt yourself or feel incompetent, and it is during these invaluable times that you should slow down and trust yourself. Trust your instincts. Take a chance, just as you ask your clients to do.

I also learned it is critical to *be* with your clients – rather than focused on *doing*. When I was present with my own emotional experiences in the therapy room, it created moments of safety where I took risks to be my authentic self and share a connection with clients. Isomorphically, there is a similar process for our clients in therapy – family members learn to *be* with one another, rather than focused on *fixing*.

Being a therapist is tough; it is hard work. There is an incredible amount of pressure to be effective when we sit across from couples and families who are hurting. We hear how difficult it is for our clients to make progress. We walk with clients through the scariness of it all. We feel their emotions with them. It is through this process that we grow special bonds with our clients. And, that is, in itself, effective. Despite a cultural emphasis on professional competence, and a potential felt need for therapists to "have it all together," therapists are, in fact, human. But to honor and be present to sharing emotional experiences with our clients is sharing our humanity and a deep connection. It was during these invaluable times that I was able to be successful with Laurie and Rob. When I felt defeated, but learned how to slow down and simply be present with what was happening in the therapy room, I was more able to explore and identify their process. I was capable of serving witness to their grief, and my own loss, and move through this pain therapeutically. In sum, we cannot expect our clients to be vulnerable if we ourselves are not willing.

2

WAYLAID SECRETS AND WELL-INTENDED PROTECTIONS

The Power of Secret-Keeping in Couples Therapy

Bron Kronborg

Supervision Issues by Connie S. Cornwell

In those early years of becoming a therapist, self-of-the-therapist issues occur frequently. Interns will be confronted with themes and presenting problems that can blur the boundaries between the intern's issues and issues that belong to the clients. In helping the intern to be aware of these possible "interface" issues, the supervisor needs to be aware of the therapist's own story. As in Bron's case, he realized one of the couple's issues, secret-keeping, had some similarity to his own. During supervision, Bron shared the role secrets played in his life and the resulting pain it had caused him. I was able to support him to realize that the *challenge* that comes with facing familiar issues could be balanced by drawing on his own understanding and discovered *strengths*, allowing him to connect with this couple.

At the same time, with little experience doing therapy, it can be difficult for the beginning therapist to trust the progress. Sometimes therapy appears as if all is going well, only to have a session where everything has regressed. A new therapist may become discouraged, work harder to fix the problem, feel inadequate, and may even blame the clients. The process of healing may not look the same for every family or couple. The two steps forward, one step back rate of improvement can keep the intern confused about whether they, and their clients, are making progress. As the old saying goes, "it may get worst before gets better." Compounding this uncertainty may be the process of using a new therapy model. A new therapist, with a therapeutic approach novel to them, may ask, *Does this model work for me? Can I learn it?* Trying on the fit of a new family or couple therapy model makes trusting that the therapeutic goal can be achieved even more difficult. It was important to support Bron to remain steadfast to the new model he was learning, Emotionally Focused Couple Therapy (EFT; Johnson, 2005), and reassure him of the effectiveness of its therapeutic process. I validated for him that it was ok *not* to trust the model until he had gained more experience using it.

During this case, Bron was challenged by the continuous introduction of new content, some of which revealed past trauma. The new content demanded attention and sometimes changed the course of therapy and a new therapeutic process emerged. This shift required the therapist to be flexible and alter directions, which was at times scary and uncomfortable. Thus, processing these concerns became one focus of my supervision with Bron and I offered live supervision. This supervision approach allowed me to support Bron in facing his discomfort and build his confidence, while taking on the challenge of learning the new model.

Further, it is a goal of mine, as a supervisor, to reinforce that people are not their disease, emotions, thoughts, or history. When feeling the boundary blur between what is a client's issue and what is the therapist's, new therapists may get quickly, and powerfully, caught up in the client's content. At these times, I remind the therapist that illnesses, diagnoses, relational problems, family issues, and life challenges are phenomena we all get to experience as human beings and, more importantly, that we are greater than the condition(s) we are presently living in. This holds true for both the therapist and the families we serve.

Bron witnessed that change was not linear – it was at times circular, deviating, recursive, and unintentional. He grew to be patient with the clients' breakdowns, and their times of breakthroughs, and was able to see the bigger picture of how therapy is a process over time, albeit a bumpy one. Lastly, Bron learned that helping clients process struggles, fears, and failings could replicate his own process of becoming a therapist.

Waylaid Secrets and Well-Intended Protections

At the time of this case I was a doctoral student intern. I was also (am still) a father, a husband, and a military veteran. I grew up surrounded by a family that was full of love and support, and that celebrated diverse spiritual faiths and ethnicities. My father is originally from Brazil, but attended medical school at Georgetown where he joined the US Air Force. He felt it important for our family to share empathy and grow up with the consistency of familiar places, people, and support. I grew up, for the most part, on a large ranch in the Sooner State. As a kid, I would often pretend that the endless prairie grassland was an African Savannah waiting for me to explore or maybe escape from everyday life. Living much of my younger life in Oklahoma, I experienced many small-town pros and cons, some of which was familiarity I still crave at times, as well as the prejudices that come with rural life.

I lived in Oklahoma until joining the USAF my senior of college. During my enlistment in the USAF, I experienced a life-changing loss, on multiple levels, as I lost my son, who passed unexpectedly. Despite being surrounded by many caring people, I felt alone. I received sympathy for my loss, instead of empathy. The organization was telling me, "don't wear your heart on your shoulder," and that it "will be okay," or that, "time takes care of everything." Sample trite statements of concern that, in fact, disconnect others from our experience.

My family appeared not to know how to handle my loss and, in fact, aided me to sweep my grief under the rug. My father, for example, had always wanted so much to make me happy. Thus, I found myself hiding my sadness around him to protect his feelings. Meanwhile, I was missing the laughter, pitter-patter of little feet, and the touch of my son. Spiritually, I felt "broken," and as a partner I felt inadequate.

From that point on, I knew my goal was to become a family therapist. I wanted to help others feel less alone, and to aid family members in being present for one another when they are at their most vulnerable. I especially wanted to support people in times when family roles or rules change due to loss.

Beginning as a Family Therapist

As a new therapist, one of my fears was being overwhelmed by a new role that would require the ability to make grounded decisions based on my education, experience, and ethical responsibilities, while also balancing the needs of the clients. Questions about self-disclosure also came up, including, *What if they ask me something personal? How much do I share? Is it important to share an experience if it benefits the client?* I was also worried about how to be both current and knowledgeable about applicable laws and the code of ethics, while maintaining my own values and simultaneously working to "fit" as a client's therapist.

Part of what helped to ground me was appraising both my capabilities and my areas for growth. One of the first questions I was asked by my internship supervisor was, "What are your strengths as a beginning therapist?" I had already learned, through coursework, that some of my strengths were being able to engage clients by keeping calm, conveying empathy, and thoughtful listening. My training had taught me the importance of giving each client time to speak while also being thoughtful of what was being said and giving value to each client's perception through questioning and clarification of the client's presenting concerns. Another question I was asked included, "What are your growing edges as a new family therapist?" It was clear my developing areas would include engaging the client through probing questions to learn more about their biopsychosocial history, contextual factors, and their resiliency in order to develop effective treatment goals based on the larger picture.

This energy of being a beginning therapist – fear of being overwhelmed, wanting to balance my educational and ethical knowledge with being present for the client, and wanting to maximize my strengths while enhancing my ability to go deep with clients – was what I carried into my work with Emily and Matt. I also carried my family-of-origin experiences, my profound loss, and my intense need to care for people when they are at their most vulnerable.

Initiating the Therapeutic Relationship

Emily and Matt were one of my first assignments during my second semester of internship – a young married couple, in their late twenties, seeking therapy that would include a spiritual acknowledgment of their faith in God and in each other. Matt was a medical professional while Emily worked at home educating their three children, ranging in ages from toddler to preteen. Although, at the start of therapy, Emily identified as a stay-at-home parent, she also expressed plans of pursuing a master's degree in a legal field with hopes it would eventually lead to becoming an attorney. The couple had previously sought therapy services from a faith-based organization in which they both reported feeling shamed and blamed. This led them to stop therapy for some time before again seeking out support. As couples often do, Matt and Emily initially sought out therapy due to a lack of communication.

Before meeting the young couple, my nerves got the best of me. I was about to be assigned a couple who did not just want couples therapy – they also wanted to include spirituality. I asked myself, *Can I meet their expectations? Can I include spirituality in therapy? Will it help me to gain rapport?* While I maintain strong aspects of spirituality in my own life, I do not practice faith-based therapy, and I was nervous about how to ethically meet this couple's needs. To get a better "feel" for who they were and how to best support them, I reached out by phone before their first appointment. The phone call was very vague: each spouse expressed little about why they were seeking couple therapy. This increased my feelings of self-doubt and anxiety: *Did I not ask the right questions over the phone? Did they not like my voice? Did I sound too clinical?* Prior to having been assigned to this couple, Matt had completed an initial intake session with a different therapist, after initiating therapy at the request of his wife. Due to scheduling conflicts, they were transferred to me. Therefore, to add to my anxiety about meeting this couple was the fact that Matt had already completed an appointment with a different provider. More concerning was that he had shared a secret in the initial session, one that he had kept from his wife for many years. He was vague in describing the secret, solely mentioning he had sexual "urges" that intimated consuming pornography. This led to more questions for the previous therapist and, now knowing the information myself, I was left with the dilemma of meeting the new client couple while knowing Matt had a deep secret that had gone on for some time.

While on the phone, and worrying I may be acting unethically by knowing, and not sharing, one partner's secret, Emily asked about my process of secret-keeping. I answered the question to the best of my ability, saying, "If either of you share something with me personally, I cannot keep that secret. I will do my best to help you discuss the secret with your partner." As she asked, I could feel a lump in my throat and heard my voice crack a little. I also wondered to myself how I could be effective, build rapport through trust, yet be sensitive to both clients, when the wife appeared to have no idea what she might be stepping into by coming to therapy. Would Matt reveal he had already expressed the secret to the other therapist? Would he give permission for me to know? Or, would it be a long process through therapy for him to share what may have been nagging at him enough to reach out for treatment?

Initiating Supervision

My concerns about Matt's secret, and how to proceed with therapy ethically, led me to meet with my clinical supervisor. I needed support and to air my self-of-the-therapist concerns so that I could provide the best clinical space for this couple. During supervision, I shared what had come up for myself – secrets kept in my previous marriage, as well as the couple's interest in spirituality, and how those things might affect how I felt toward either of the two clients. Through the work of supervision, I realized that, even though I was a new therapist who wanted the best for my clients, I was still human, with experiences that would come up when meeting with and supporting clients. I was able to talk through my concerns and ground myself in knowing I could support the clients, even knowing the husband had a secret. Together, my supervisor and I decided that transparency would be necessary to gain the trust of both clients. This meant it might take time to help the husband feel comfortable enough to reveal his secret.

My clinical supervisor and I also discussed how the couple might benefit from EFT (Johnson, 2005) due to the possible underlying trauma both clients might be experiencing. We discussed how using an EFT approach could help Matt realize his part in the couple's cycle, and why it may have been important for him to keep secrets. Conceptualizing this case through an EFT lens also helped me to understand that Emily may, in fact, know her husband's secret, but be hiding this fact due to hurt, shame, or insecurity. Because the couple had initially sought Christian marital therapy, we also decided to use their spirituality as a strength to promote resilience. We agreed this might also help to gain the couple's trust during the initial stages of rapport-building in EFT.

Because the counseling center I was interning at is at a large teaching hospital, my supervisor and I discussed the appropriateness of having medical students observe the couple's therapy. Additionally, my clinical supervisor would join most sessions and be available to help with what could be a complex case. While the thought of being observed by a group of future physicians made me anxious, I felt reassured knowing my supervisor and I would be collaborating. Lastly, my supervisor reiterated the strengths of my therapeutic style and boosted my confidence for our first session.

The First Session and Building Rapport

When I first met Matt and Emily, I felt a sense of familiarity. Though I had never met them before, we sat down and they began speaking as if we had known each other for many years. Husband and wife sat close to each other, holding hands, nervous, but both expressing a desire to be in therapy together to improve their relationship. They began the session with a prayer, which the therapy team respected by keeping silent. They both shared wonderful stories of growing up around each other in a small Texas town. They shared how they met at church as teenagers and began dating shortly after. Emily was drawn to Matt initially because he was a "rebel" and "different" than what her father would expect from a boyfriend; she was from a family with strict rules and roles. Matt reported his family had lacked structure and support. Lastly, while the couple suggested that their faith was important as a form of social support, it was evident their religious system continued to contribute to their feelings of doubt. Overall, I felt drawn to their genuine and loving stories.

About midway into the session, and very suddenly, Emily shared she was aware that Matt had had several affairs. This disclosure was unexpected and a bit shocking. As Emily described the pain she felt due to the betrayal, my heart sank. I found myself empathizing with her after all the fond memories she had shared about her husband and her marriage. My heart also went out to Matt – his face was full of pain, and he sunk down in his chair.

Much of the rest of the first session focused on the husband's secrets. He disclosed a history of sexual abuse in childhood by male perpetrators, which had led him to question his sexual orientation, and he shared about the energy he had spent hiding these secrets from his family and church. The couple also acknowledged that Emily would ask questions, at home, about Matt's trauma history. As a result, they explained, Matt often became withdrawn, which led to more infidelity and an enormous lack of trust.

The volume of what was shared in this, and the first few sessions, was exhausting. Overall, it seemed obvious that both clients loved each other and protected each other at the cost of their own self-worth. I knew this behavior well – I, too, had experienced this, while hiding my grief around others to protect their feelings.

Unraveling Secrets and Self-of-the-Therapist Reactions

While working with the couple, my supervisor and I noticed the couple had peculiar language regarding Matt's infidelity. One of the code words the couple used was "urges." While both used the term, they each appeared to have a different meaning for the word. During one session, Matt spoke about his urges and how he would pray for them to go away. He seemed to be talking about something other than just infidelity. It felt as if he wanted us to read into the meaning and to understand him, without him having to explain. When he talked about the "urges," it also seemed to bring much shame and embarrassment. His face would turn bright red and he appeared short of breath at times. He would look at me but not at his wife. Observing Matt's process in therapy brought up feelings I had had, when thinking or talking about my own sexual orientation. I understood how hard it was to talk about it, and to wish you could pray those feelings away. However, I also wanted to be careful: I did not want to read into what Matt was saying or place my own meaning on his description. I felt it was best to separate my own self-of -the-therapist issues and truly be present with the client.

Open-ended questions were asked in order to clarify the term "urges." Emily quickly answered for her husband, stating it meant, "the urge to be with someone else," as if she was still protecting him – or herself – from really learning the meaning of the word. Matt's quiet and body language, however, indicated he was unsure he was thinking the same. Thus, I asked Matt to clarify *his* definition of what "urges" meant to him. Matt was noticeably silent. Then, he shared that he sometimes had urges that involved same-sex thoughts or fantasy. Matt explained that, in many of his affairs, he would invite his female partners to be dominating in order to appease these "urges," since prayer did not work. He emphasized an assumed power differential, and that his partners were asked to be in control. He also expressed that, in a way, God was punishing him and his family for things he had done in his past, suggesting his experiences of abuse, though his descriptions of this were cryptic.

This session was a turning point. It was now clear that there was more than infidelity haunting this relationship. Due to the role Matt identified assuming in his extramarital partnerships, I wondered whether the same-sex urges came not from a question of sexual orientation, but whether they possibly evolved from Matt's being subject to sexual abuse. To help this couple, I discussed that it would be necessary to better understand Matt's same-sex attraction as well as his trauma history. If it was discovered Matt's fantasies, and infidelity, may stem from his abuse history, I felt I could help the couple work through the emotional trauma. If Matt came to understand he was gay, however, I was concerned the therapy process would be ethically risky in advocating for the couple to remain together. I decided to keep an open mind and give Matt the space necessary to discuss his meaning of sexual urges.

As therapy progressed, with Emily's permission many of our sessions attended to Matt. Emily shared that, at home, she was often busy imagining her husband's betrayal in her mind while her husband talked. She asked for help to manage these thoughts and truly be able to listen to her husband, so that she might better understand his infidelity. Thus, Emily was invited to be attentive and supportive by listening. It was evident Emily both wanted to be her husband's confidant, and needed to protect herself from the trauma she had already experienced in the relationship. She seemed to be her husband's biggest cheerleader in life; always building him up when others in their family tore him down. He occupied her heart, and I was moved by her intent to help her husband. On reflection, I was also likely caught up in protecting Matt from experiencing additional trauma from Emily's pursuit. While I focused quite a bit of time on Matt, looking back, I wish I had spent more time with Emily, too. She presented Matt as the concern, and we bought in; in truth, they were both hurting, and she likely also needed protection.

During one session, the couple arrived a little late and not their usual bubbly selves. It was apparent the couple had been arguing before coming to session. Matt was also unshaven, his clothes were rumpled, and stress was in his facial expressions. They sat apart from each other, angry. My anxiety that they did not appear to be the couple I had grown to love working with brought up other concerns for me, that I might be becoming too attached to seeing the couple succeed.

Matt spoke of the urges becoming extraordinarily strong at times, especially when he thought of his failures. When asked to go deeper into thinking about times the urges were their strongest, Matt finally, fully, opened up about the sexual trauma he had faced as a young boy, and that had continued into his adolescence. I sat and listened intently. Not saying a word, but showing empathy through being there in his moment of vulnerability.

Matt expressed sadness, shame, guilt, and anger felt from the early sexual abuse experiences. He described how older neighbor boys were the perpetrators, which lead to him becoming trapped in the abuse – he also became a perpetrator with other boys his age. He explained that he was pushed into the abuse by the older neighbors, who reinforced the behavior at school and at their shared church. Matt also expressed that perpetrating gave him some control – if he was perpetrating, he would not be hurt by others, and he had also felt more in control of his rage. He acknowledged that what he had done was wrong, but that he had felt trapped and ashamed. The neighborhood boys had all kept this dark secret for years. Matt shared that he is still friends, today, with many of them, who are now married and have children of their own. No one has ever talked about their boyhood past. My supervisor and I discussed a potential need to report these occurrences to protective services; however, there was no indication that the children of these childhood friends-turned-adults were aware of or exposed to these abuses. This couple, and many others, had learned through multiple generations to hide everything for appearance's sake.

Lastly, Matt revealed that, as an adult, he had met several men on business trips in which he would role-play his abuse. These relationships were a continuation of seeking a feeling of being in control; they met this need in the moment, but their satisfaction was very short-lived. In sum, Matt shared that it had become easier to ask for forgiveness for his infidelity than talk about all of these experiences, which were overwhelming him.

In some way, I felt I could relate to Matt wanting to hide his childhood secrets. I did not experience abuse, but I experimented, sexually, with friends my age, and carried a great deal of shame in this, the feelings that resulted, and about my sexual orientation. My own religious experiences promoted my guilt, and resulted in my maintaining my identity as a secret for many years.

I decided it was now time to ask Matt if he questioned his sexual orientation or felt he was gay. Matt reported he did not feel attracted to men, but instead to the act of subsiding his guilt and shame. I felt washed in relief, and realized I was getting caught up in rooting for this marriage to succeed. I also realized I did not want him to endure the negative social experiences that come with being gay. Matt looked so defeated, like a little boy, sobbing and in need of comfort. As Emily reached out and hugged him, I felt tearful, but hid my emotions to not interfere with the couple relating to each other in the moment.

After this revelation from Matt, I determined I would trust that sexual orientation was not the concern. I conceptualized the sexual trauma as the driving force of his avoidance in the couple's cycle. However, for Emily, learning of her husband's abuse history was not comforting. It, instead, led to more questions, fears, and hurt. Emily expressed she had been her husband's best friend for years, only to find out now, with us, that he had hidden this from her. It appeared that knowing about the infidelity was easier than knowing about the trauma. Emily also shared how she felt inadequate as a partner in not being someone that her husband wanted to share this information with. Her feelings of defeat were evident. This was especially hard for me, because I had kept my sexual orientation a secret from my ex-wife. I thought about how my ex-wife must have felt when I confirmed her fears. This couple also now consisted of two very hurt individuals; both had a need for reassurance of their personhood, but their unique flavors of insecurity were now somewhat at odds, complicating therapy.

Progress through EFT

As the therapy process continued, much progress was made with Matt in helping him come to terms with the trauma he had experienced and making sense of why he had become avoidant in his marriage. He started to trust, and began leaning on his wife to share his feelings. As Matt began the healing process, therapy began to focus more on Emily and the trauma she experienced through learning of her husband's affairs. Additionally, much of the work through EFT centered around the couple's cycle of pursue and withdraw. Matt had been the withdrawer due to the shame of his secrets, while Emily had pursued him for answers. Emily often spoke of how even little emotions that occurred would trigger her and cause her to pursue. She shared stories of how she and Matt would be driving, running errands, or out to have fun, and her mind would begin to think about her mistrust of him, or how she blamed herself. She described these experiences as debilitating, at times, taking her away from her daily life. Emily's negative thought patterns would become all-consuming, and she would begin to provoke her husband, seeking answers at all costs.

Through the process of EFT, however, Matt and Emily began to come to the realization that, no matter how many questions were asked, or how much information was learned, the answers did not satisfy Emily's need. I framed Emily's questioning of her husband, in part, as a behavior that may have developed from her own past family-of-origin experiences of emotional abuse and small-town family secrets. Both partners had grown up not being able to share their traumas. But, keeping them a secret perpetuated the couple's cycle. Thus, much of the healing process in therapy centered around the couple's ability to gain trust, and to have faith that their partner would always stand by them, even in disagreement.

The End and Then Not So Much

Eventually, we neared the couple's last session. Matt and Emily had been a part of my life, sharing their vulnerability, for nearly 18 months. The last session was an emotional one. Hugs and tears were shared while discussing their therapy experience. As the couple left that day, I remember having an "end of summer camp" feeling. The knowing you might not ever again see the people whom you had grown to care for and enjoy. That sadness you feel in your chest when saying goodbye and the not knowing what the future has in store for the people with whom you've shared emotions, vulnerability, and laughter. As with most clients, the door was kept open for the couple to continue therapy if needed.

As the summer passed, I did, once again, hear from the couple. Emily called to see if I could meet with them, and expressed that she and her husband were in fight-or-flight mode; she feared they were falling apart. I consulted with my supervisor and we weighed the possibility of enabling versus supporting the couple; it was decided to meet with them and evaluate the crisis. During the crisis meeting, I learned that neither partner had exposed all their secrets during therapy. The couple revealed that they had both agreed to involve a third person in their sexual relationship, which had caused much turmoil during their absence from therapy. Emily expressed how Matt often requested she meet with different people, often male, so that he could take part in the experience. Emily assented to these relationships to appease Matt, and discussed the couple's religious beliefs as part of her agreement to participate. However, Emily described these sexual experiences as humiliating and enabling Matt's "urges," stacking more trauma and pain on the relationship.

My heart sank for both. I had so many mixed emotions during this crisis session. I felt betrayed and inadequate as a therapist and even, possibly, as a friend. I had assumed I had built trust, while wanting this couple to succeed. I realized then that maybe this was my dilemma. Maybe I had been caught up in being the couple's biggest fan, wanting the therapy process to "succeed," that I did not give them the space they needed to be fully transparent. It was an eye-opener for me. I felt, intensely, my human need to please others. The shame of disappointing someone affected me, as well as the couple.

A second revelation was just as heartbreaking. The couple disclosed that Matt had lost his job and they were financially unable to continue living in their home. They were going to give up their home and move in with Matt's family. I was confused. The story they had portrayed during therapy was that Matt's family was distant and removed from their lives. In fact, the opposite was true: Matt's family had been financially supportive to the couple for years. With this upcoming relocation, they also shared it would no longer be feasible to attend therapy. However, it was agreed they would attend four sessions in the period leading up to their move.

During our final four sessions, focus was on the trust Matt and Emily had built in their work together, and the transparency they had had with each other. While I wanted them to succeed, and looked forward to meeting with them, my enthusiasm felt distant. I was possibly protecting myself, and my own feelings, by not getting too attached to the couple or their outcome. I realized that my own process, as a therapist, required me to take care of myself while being able to provide the clients with a space to be vulnerable. As the final session ended, it was, once again, hard for me to say goodbye. We had spent almost a year and a half together, learning one another's body language, vocal intonations, and facial cues, and each of us had been vulnerable.

Conclusion

My initial fear when starting internship, the unknown — what clients I would be assigned, what they would come in with, what I might need to help clients be successful — has faded with time. Instead, ending these sessions with Matt and Emily, and my first use of EFT, left me asking, *How will I make sure to take care of myself as a therapist?* I think this is probably easier said than accomplished. Much of my self-care during this case relied on the ability to be transparent with my supervisor. I was able to disclose to her my stresses, and my need to trust my clinical self, as well as my goal to develop my ability to compartmentalize my self-of-the-therapist reactions and remain present with both partners through reflective listening. My supervisor highlighted that my role at home as a father, and my abilities as a natural caregiver, could be helpful in learning how to take care of myself as a therapist while also relating to the needs of my clients.

We need those distractions and coping skills. I found that, no matter how much we think the client's experience will not affect us, sudden self-of-the-therapist reactions will come up and surprise us. This experience can affect our personal relationships with friends, family, and partners. As with my military training, I learned that the little things we take for granted need to have importance. Basics like eating, drinking plenty of fluids, and getting rest. Sometimes just being able to take a shower without being disturbed does much for a fresh mind and perspective. It can also serve as "washing off the day." I learned it was critical for me to take time out from my own family to take care of myself, even if only for a few minutes.

As with any relationship in life – friend, acquaintance, or client – saying goodbye is never easy. I am, in fact, a human, that happens to be a therapist, with real emotion. Thus, still today, I think of this couple. I spent so much time with them, and experienced so many of my own vulnerabilities during the course of their treatment. Some of this still washes over me when I remember our experience or wonder about their outcome. Learning to stay aware of my self-of-the-therapist reactions through my work with Matt and Emily has helped me to become more cognizant of when to lean on supervisors and emphasize self-care. Therapists are going to feel the emotions that come up in the therapy room – vulnerability, anxiety, fear – and we cannot sweep our own grief under the rug. Our work is, instead, to pursue our own growth and learn to trust ourselves.

Part I Conclusion

Both of the couples described in Part I proved to be powerfully impactful for each of these therapists. Though their secrets were, at first, overwhelming, each intern learned to reflect on their own internal experiences, consider their self-of-the-therapist reactions, and move more intentionally into the therapeutic space. These cases demonstrate the dance of clients with one another, the dance between clients and therapist, and the dance of the therapist and their own relationships – like a successive twirl, the spinning of one subsystem can create progress in the others. The rippling impacts of each indicate that change can begin anywhere.

In addition to the impacts on clients and therapists-in-training, the supervisory system was actively involved in both cases, each of which was uniquely challenging. This also highlights the importance of a supervisor debriefing with other supervisors – connecting with supervisor colleagues about the hard work, soliciting input on whether there is anything else they could have done. It can be critically important for supervisors to get clarity on the work they're doing, and that can especially come from inviting a peer's input. Another example of the power of expanding the system!

Thought Questions

1. How do you know when to ask for help with a case? How many cases are you seeing, or have you seen, where you have needed help but held back? Why did you hold back?
2. How do you deal with the situation when clients question your age, training, marital status, or your ability to handle their case? Have you ever felt your clients were judging your ability, but they did not mention this to you? How does this impact your confidence? Do you find yourself making more references about being under supervision with these cases?
3. When self-of-therapist issues come up, are you comfortable talking about these issues with your supervisor? How do you discover these overlaps, and how do you bring them up? What

benefits have you experienced of processing self-of-the-therapist reactions in supervision?

4. How do you prepare to use a new theoretical model in your clinical work? When using a model you have less experience with, do you ask for guidance or do you think you should master it on your own? How do you ensure the competence of your work when using a new model?

5. Can you identify diffuse or rigid boundaries, and how they impact family rules around privacy?

6. With which of your current (or past) clients would it be helpful to identify isomorphic processes? How can/could you use your understanding of isomorphism as an intervention in this case?

7. How does your family-of-origin handle secrets? How might this impact your work with clients who have painful secrets and hidden traumas?

Part II

FAMILY THERAPY AND OUTSIDE SYSTEMS

A Slippery Slope

Introduction to Part II

Cases that involve multiple agencies, or mental health professionals with different agendas, are complex and can be very challenging. They can also be highly rewarding, especially as the family therapist may serve as the sole provider envisioning the many players in a big-picture conceptualization of the case. This bird's eye view of the patient(s), the family, and the many other systems within which they're embedded, especially collaborating treatment providers, may also require the family therapist to serve in the role of advocate. To be the client's voice in an oft overwhelming and complicated network of stakeholders. Thus, the supervisor's role is, first, to help the intern shift to larger-systems thinking, beyond just the family. In other words, extending new family therapists' systemic conceptualizing to include the macrosystems clients are embedded in, as well as the interactions across systems' levels. Second, the supervisor should prioritize preserving the therapist's well-being, enhancing their confidence, and boosting their immunity to the contagious nature of pathologizing, individualizing, and isolation.

Family Therapy Models and Larger Systems

Several family therapy theories address the role of systems external to the patient, their family, and the work of family therapy. Examples include narrative and medical family therapy approaches.

Narrative Therapy

The crux of narrative therapy is rooted in social constructionism, an epistemology that explains how the many aspects of a culture are co-created by the members of that society as they connect and interact with one another, linguistically, over time. These constructed norms, values, mores, and practices are lenses through which individuals view and understand their world (Freedman & Combs, 1996). This postmodern philosophy influenced narrative therapy, such that the model emphasizes how societal norms impact and inform the stories families live and create. When families operate in opposition to prevailing beliefs or customs (dominant narratives), their lived experience may be powerfully framed by these sociocultural influences, and overtaken by limiting problem-saturated narratives. In turn, the explanations that clients tell themselves about their problems affect families' self-perceptions. In other words, families' narratives are not solely descriptive, but are constitutive; they shape experience in their telling and retelling (White & Epston, 1990). In order to therapeutically address these problem-saturated stories, narrative therapists directly address, question, and challenge the culture's values and ideas, in order to co-construct with clients an alternative, preferred story line. The goal is, first, to promote alternative ways of clients' viewing themselves and their problems, and to engage clients in envisioning struggling against their problems, now externalized. Second, narrative therapists emphasize how dominant narratives become internalized stories, and maintain a goal of clients' extricating themselves from this oppression.

In regards to Part II's focus on external systems, narrative therapy can be a powerful therapeutic approach to highlighting for families the impact of larger systems they are nested within. Specifically, practitioners of this model would attend to and question the belief systems of clients' larger systems, discuss the impact of these systems on the family's beliefs about themselves and their identified problem, and open space to create new meanings and stories that promote preferred selves (Freedman & Combs, 1996).

Medical Family Therapy

A second family therapy approach that derives directly from larger-systems work is *medical family therapy* (McDaniel, Doherty, & Hepworth, 2014). Medical family therapy utilizes systems theory (von Bertalanffy, 1968) and the biopsychosocial model (Engel, 1977, 1980) to inform clinical work conducted collaboratively in healthcare systems. The biopsychosocial model, similarly derived from general systems theory, was developed in response to the prevailing biomedical model utilized in healthcare. The model specifies the interconnections between each hierarchical level of a patient's system, beginning at the subatomic and ending with the biosphere. Each level of a patient's system is organized and responsive, while simultaneously being nested within higher, larger levels of the system; inter-systemic influence is negotiated by boundaries between each level (Engel, 1980).

Specific to family therapy applications, McDaniel et al. (2014) utilized the biopsychosocial model to inform their medical family therapy approach, which was originated to promote the integration of mind and body; individual patient and family; family and institutional settings; the clinical, financial, and operational worlds of healthcare (Peek, 2008); and, medicine with the community context. In other words, medical family therapists specifically work to expand their lens, and the lens of the healthcare team, to incorporate considerations of each of these realms into treatment. Through facilitating integration, and promoting communication and collaboration between patients and families, between family systems and medical staff, and between medical and mental health providers, medical family therapists are able to encourage whole-person care while discouraging isolation.

Lastly, two primary goals of medical family therapy include increasing agency, especially in regard to empowering patients and families to take an active voice and make decisions about their health and healthcare, and enhancing communion, or the support and collaboration of family and community. These goals also apply to work with larger systems – specifically, medical family therapists may work to promote the agency of underpowered medical staff and support alternate mental health providers in giving voice to their own goals and specific approaches of healing families. Additionally, they may work to help the healthcare team feel supported, addressing burnout, professional rifts, territorial behavior, siloed providers, and isolation. Most recently, clinical competencies for family therapists working in healthcare settings have been specified (American Association of Marriage and Family Therapy, 2018). These include, among others, the importance of facilitating inter-system communication, developing medical literacy, responding to intersecting needs of the healthcare system, and advocating for integrated care via healthcare policy.

Supervisory Interventions to Extend Systems Thinking

Deriving from these and other approaches, supervisors will likely need to address new therapists' competency in working with external systems head-on. As supervisees are working with individual families, they need to learn how to stand back and take a larger systems view that includes all other professionals. They need to be able to see everyone involved in the case as a family member in the large system, and especially be aware of differing agendas. The ultimate goal, therapeutically, is to maintain rapport with larger systems and other providers involved in the family's care, while healing the identified problem.

Systems Mapping

To begin in supervision with multiple-stakeholder cases, it helps to map out the larger system, often drawing it in order to diagram all those involved in the case – their connections, affiliations, roles, treatment goals, and agendas. Similar to a traditional genogram (and as an extension of cultural genograms used in healthcare settings; Shellenberger et al., 2007), these systemic maps can include relational lines between the various members to highlight the quality of connections, whether close, distant, or absent. The purpose is to ensure the learner has a clear understanding of each level of the client's hierarchy, who

specifically is involved, and how each person or organization is partici-
pating. This process may help to illuminate potential conflicts, relational
triangles, and discordant treatment goals that may stunt therapeutic
progress, confuse families about their true objectives, and erode systemic buy-in to the family therapy process.

Circular Questioning

After mapping the patient and family within the larger system's hierarchy, the supervisor can ask questions to enhance the trainee's larger-
systems view and ability to take alternate perspectives. The goal of this
supervisory process would be to expand the therapist's case conceptualization to consider and incorporate other angles and stakeholders'
emphases. Much like circular, relational questions in family therapy,
the supervisor can ask questions such as: Who does that provider
answer to; how does that influence their approach? What personal
goals might they have for this family; are any unspoken? What do they
understand about what you do and what your role is with this family?
Have they bought into your treatment goals; why or why not? What
might they be afraid of? Why do you think this patient's behavior
increases that organization's anxiety? If you were to share your secret
hopes for these clients with that provider, how do you think they might
react?

The process invites the therapist to give the other systems involved
the benefit of the doubt, and to acknowledge and recognize the
potential positive outcomes that may come from staying collaboratively
engaged. Developing empathy for these external, but very much
involved, "family members" allows the therapist the flexibility to dance
between systems, rather than just within the family system. It also
allows them to see the large whole, centered around an identified
problem.

Advocacy Ethics and a Social Justice Lens

In the vein of building families' agency, supervisors may also wish to
emphasize the ethics of family therapists' advocacy for their patients.
Promoting clients' agency does not negate the need for the therapist to

give voice to clients' wishes in complicated or denigrating systems. Working together with, or on behalf of, client families to combat oppressive dominant narratives can be a critically important component of the work, and may be especially informed using a social justice lens.

Thus, supervisors can work to sensitize therapists and attune them to power dynamics in their cases, externally involved systems, and larger sociocultural contexts (McDowell, Knudson-Martin, & Bermudez, 2019). Further, they can discuss unique approaches to the ethics of advocacy defined by differing theoretical approaches and identify specific therapeutic interventions to position clients in their social systems. Interventions may include the use of therapist transparency; curious inquiry through the use of good client-centered questions; and naming for families the unjust influences of sociocultural policies and contexts on their lives (D'Arrigo-Patrick, Hoff, Knudson-Martin, & Tuttle, 2017; McDowell et al., 2019). Further, new therapists can explore clients' struggles, "staying experience near," rather than solely identifying what a theoretical model might conceptualize as a problem's origin; conduct explicit social education and raise clients' awareness; or, practice tentativeness and meet clients where they're at (D'Arrigo-Patrick et al., 2017, p. 580). Supervisors can also encourage their learners to intervene by emphasizing the value of clients' strengths in order to counter oppressive dominant narratives that invalidate these traits (McDowell et al., 2019).

Enhancing new therapists' ability to situate clients (and therapy) in complicated networks of power dynamics, while advocating for and with clients, reflects third-order thinking (McDowell et al., 2019). Specifically, this type of supervision assists supervisees with recognizing power and how it is important (Knudson-Martin, 2013), supporting equity across theoretical approaches, and actively intervening in the social contexts and societal processes families (and supervisees) are nested in (McDowell, Knudson-Martin, & Bermudez, 2018, 2019). Lastly, the interventions above are not enough to create third-order change. As McDowell et al. (2019) emphasize, therapists must facilitate families considering alternatives and imagining other solutions they might attempt if openly addressing problematic power dynamics in their spheres. In the supervision process, supervisors can also engage trainees in envisioning alternatives to their therapeutic interventions, how they might give voice to their clients' needs in other systems, and what it would look like to candidly grapple with power.

Role-Play

Taking a larger-systems view, collaborating with professionals operating from different paradigms, and addressing inter-system power dynamics can be intimidating prospects for new therapists. Thus, supervisees may benefit from experiential practice in supervision to help them feel prepared. The use of role-play in supervision can assist supervisees with taking multiple perspectives – playing the part of therapist, family member, and community agency facilitates taking on and valuing disparate viewpoints, as well as growing empathy. Further, rehearsing conversations with collaborators can enhance supervisees' sense of preparation and confidence, and support their ability to join and advocate with external systems.

Overall, the use of these, and other, supervision interventions can promote supervisees' understanding of the systemic assumption of *equifinality*. New family therapists may struggle to understand the value of collaboration and the importance of respecting varied treatment perspectives, but specifically emphasizing that there are many routes to the same goal may enhance their overall systemic thinking. Further, it may help engage supervisees in considering whether they, the family, and other providers have, in fact, the same end goal in mind.

Lastly, it is the supervisor's duty to ensure the health and well-being of the therapist-in-training. When the therapist's struggles are dominated by tension or hostility in the workplace, it is necessary to help the learner recognize the impact of this environment, and support the therapist moving on to a new setting. Even with our best efforts at being affiliative and collaborative, it is sometimes appropriate to listen to systems that may be telling us they are not ready for change.

Preventing the Therapist from Catching the Disease

External systems' emphases on the individual patient can quickly overshadow a therapist's systemic perspective. However, new therapists can be trained to attune to "individualistic and pathologizing systems at work … [and] respectfully interrupt them" on clients' behalves (McDowell et al., 2019, p. 19). Similarly, supervisors should attend to when these systems infect their supervisee's thinking, and provide the systemic antidote. For the beginning therapist, it is easy to get caught in this dominant narrative, especially if it is the pervasive view of other mental health professionals involved.

The ability to inoculate oneself against individualistic, problem-saturated, or hopeless paradigms may increase with confidence. While younger therapists may be coached to "fake it 'til you make it," to rehearse taking on a shroud of self-assuredness, second career interns may be more successful at this out of the gate. Supervisees with prior professional lives may have wisdom and savvy, and be quicker to embrace the mantle of professionalism. They may also be, therefore, more observant of collaborating (or co-located) mental health professionals' gaps in care and training differences, and thus less willing to put up with the status quo. Thankfully, senior interns with a strong personal sense of worth may also be less afraid to sit in a room with other professionals and advocate for their families. They can step forward and take charge with confidence and assertiveness in dealing with other professionals in the larger system.

Thus, in addition to supervisors' interventions to grow new therapists' abilities to not catch the pathologizing disease, younger supervisees can also learn from confident, later career colleagues. Learners with life experience and assertiveness can teach, model, and remind younger trainees how to walk and talk as a professional and feel confident. Through intentional, or unintentional, pairings between first and second (or higher-order) career interns, younger learners can learn intentionally about presence – especially important in the face of strong, overpowering clients, or similarly flavored large systems.

3

SYSTEMS WITHIN SYSTEMS
Collaboration and Therapeutic Strategies for Navigating Chaos

Laurie Poole

Supervision Issues by Connie S. Cornwell

Cases can be complex and overwhelming for the supervisor, too. *How do I help the intern manage the complexity of so many other professionals involved in the case?* As the family grows larger and more complicated, it can be challenging for interns to balance the many systems' competing demands. It can also be difficult for the supervisor who may, at times, be weighing political concerns and the need to tread lightly for the protection of the intern or the clinic. As described above, mapping the system is helpful in showing the many connections – this is true for both supervisee and supervisor.

Size and number are not the only factors that confound therapy with larger-systems clients. Often a case is complicated due to the referral source. In Laurie's case, externally involved providers were prescribing a behavioral approach that was creating more conflict and stress for the family. My job, as the supervisor, was to support Laurie in keeping rapport with the referral source, while preventing the other treatment from sabotaging the family therapy work. It was a challenge and, at times, overwhelming. This work, and all therapy with outside stakeholders, requires larger-systems thinking – everyone involved in the case was seen as a client. Consequently, the treatment need was to be therapeutic to all.

Systems within Systems

Have you ever felt overwhelmed and underqualified by a situation that feels bigger than your therapeutic capacity to contribute? That was me when I was presented with a complex case of dynamics involving two children within a blended family. We often joked at the family therapy center where I interned that the universe delivers clients who teach us what we need to learn. Despite my own considerable life experience, I was about to learn in spades.

At the time I first met with the Curtis family, I was in the first year of working through postgraduate licensure hours and was older than most of my interning colleagues. Becoming a therapist was a third act career; I had enjoyed successful careers in higher education and the corporate world, and had been married twice with grown children of my own. I was no stranger to stress, having experienced serious illness, the death of loved ones, unemployment, career changes, and parenting challenges. Having lived a laboratory of life experiences, I felt more than ready when I started a master's program in counseling.

I have always been the go-to person when colleagues and friends need someone to confide in, but it was a different game sitting in a therapist's chair. The weightiness of responsibility and the fear of screwing up a client were issues I had to process over time. And as I think back, I am not sure that I was entirely transparent about my fears, or the discomfort I felt of no longer being an "expert" in my field. It was humbling to acknowledge that there was much to learn and that I could not possibly know "everything."

As fate would have it, by the time this case came into the center, I was the more senior intern and the most likely candidate to take it on. My supervisor explained that it was a referral from the nearby children's hospital and a complex case, but she knew I could handle it. Truth be told, it was far more complex than initially presented and it did not take long to feel intimidated by a chaotic family system with two children caught in the eye of the storm. With many players in the case – two sets of parents and their partners, three sets of grandparents, school counselors and administrators, mental health professionals, CPS, and the court system – I felt overwhelmed and lost. *What could I possibly offer this family? Where should I start and with whom?* I felt like an imposter, sure that I would be called out for my lack of experience. Like my clients, I, too, became intimidated by the number of "experts" casting influence over this family.

A rule follower by nature, this is the story of how chaos and the challenge of authority contributed to my own metamorphosis as a therapist.

Introducing the Curtis Family

Two members of the Curtis Family – Kyle, age 11 and Kayla, age 6 – were referred by a local children's hospital for family therapy, and served as the "identified patients." Their parents, Mary, age 36, and Alex, age 37, had divorced two years prior; each parent subsequently remarried. At the time, Mary was given primary custody. Mary cohabited with Glen, age 42, whose 11-year-old daughter Cassie visited every other weekend. Alex had married Barbara, age 31, also previously married with two children, Kendra, age 7, and Jamie, age 5, who lived with them full-time.

Kyle and Kayla's custody agreement changed within a year of their parents' divorce. A complaint of suspected neglect was filed by Kyle's school counselor, resulting in a CPS investigation. Kyle had complained to a teacher that he had no food to eat and was kicked out of the house with no jacket. Additional issues surfaced suggesting that Mary also struggled with managing the children's behavior. Alex subsequently filed for, and won, primary custody of Kyle and Kayla, who then went to live with him, Barbara, and Barbara's two children. I was to later learn that, in the course of the complaint, Alex never approached Mary to discuss or validate Kyle's complaints, which set the scene for animosity and bitterness between the former spouses and their new partners.

As Kyle and Kayla were acting out when living with their mom, CPS recommended a series of medical and psychological evaluations.

Post-Traumatic Stress Disorder, Oppositional Defiant Disorder, and Attention-Deficit/Hyperactivity Disorder were each diagnosed for both children, medications were prescribed, and it was subsequently recommended they enroll in a summer-long behavioral day treatment program at the area children's hospital. When the day treatment was completed, the attending psychologist recommended family and play therapies as follow-up treatments. Additionally, the children were to continue working on "behavioral compliance and self-control" by following a reward-based behavioral program managed at home by Alex and Barbara, under the direction of the hospital psychologist. Simply described, Kyle and Kayla's behavior was evaluated daily and charted primarily by their stepmom, as she was home during the day. She logged whether homework was completed, whether chores were carried out, whether dinner was eaten before dessert, and how quickly the children responded. This at-home behavioral program was administered to Barbara's two children, as well, to make the rules consistent for all. Depending on their success for meeting behavioral goals, the children (all four) gained or lost privileges.

The program and recommended treatment became a key player in the family system. The more I heard about its demands, the more it felt like swatting a fly with a hammer. Not many adults could tolerate such scrutiny of their behavior, never mind children. I could not understand how a rigorous regimen of check marks and charts was going to bring this family together. But, I had to figure a way to work with "it" and provide support, and used family therapy sessions as a conduit for what the behavior management program could never provide – love and connection.

Initiating Care

I remember my first meeting with Kyle and Kayla, who came in with their dad and stepmom for a family session. They were a little timid and uncertain, but there was something about Kyle to which I was particularly drawn. He was a cocky, curious, smooth-talking boy who held strong opinions about his role in the family turmoil. His strategic protests would later create heightened chaos to make the adults pay attention to his cries for love and acceptance. He was a truth-teller, a whistle-blower.

His younger, quieter sister, Kayla, looked to Kyle for approval. As the family ship's captain, stepmom Barbara did most of the talking while dad, Alex, chimed in occasionally. I was initially impressed by how invested Barbara seemed to be in Alex's children – she completed all the intake documents, knew their diagnoses and medications, tracked their schedules and treatment plans. She worked hard at managing the family while her husband appeared happy for her to be the "expert" parent. I found myself wondering why Alex handed over the reins, when he had fought so hard to gain custody of his children. In our first few sessions, I listened empathetically to Alex's story of the custody battle for his children; how uncooperative and resistant their mother was; how Kyle and Kayla's acting out behaviors at school increased; and the all-consuming role the behavior management program played at home – the most disturbing piece of the case, for me. The anxiety level within the family system was palpable.

Each week, Barbara and Alex reported on the success rate of Kyle and Kayla's compliance with an exhausting hypervigilance. Each session opened with a rundown of ways in which Kyle was disobedient, didn't listen, and didn't care about consequences for his behavior. It felt oppressive and heavy. While I understood that he could be difficult and disruptive, I felt increasingly protective of Kyle, as I recognized a boy with wisdom and insight, who longed for love and acceptance. His parents appeared emotionally checked out during sessions, with an intense focus on their children's compliance.

Emotions other than anger and frustration were tough to access amongst family members. As hard as I tried to steer the session away from a focus on complaints about Kyle, I felt powerless and intimidated. It was hard to remain open and curious as I witnessed how the family clung to a vice grip of immobility. The more the children protested the checks and balances of the system, the tighter the reins were held by the parents, particularly by Barbara, who felt powerless and lost.

This program was supposed to make things better, but from the therapist's chair, all I could see was that it made things worse. The relationship between Barbara and Alex became strained, while Kyle expressed his frustration with his father by intentionally breaking every family rule. Barbara verbally, and resentfully, protested her being left to manage – not parent or assist with, but "manage" – his children's behavior.

Tearfully, Barbara complained that she was always the "bad guy"; she was desperate for her husband's support and involvement in parenting. Why did Alex abdicate leadership with his children and withdraw while Barbara pushed in pursuit of family peace? There was more to this than was coming out in therapy. I began to recognize Alex's passivity as a red flag, and decided it was time to unpack it, and dig deeper by working with family subgroups.

Breaking It Down

Several weeks into therapy, it became clear that Kyle was the focus of numerous sessions. Behavior escalated at home and at school, with temper tantrums and acting out behavior. His misbehavior, noncompliance, and protests were a source of frustration for his parents. With such an intense focus on Kyle, I couldn't get a clear picture of the children's relationship with their dad, unless I saw the three of them as a subsystem. I was curious about the effects of an abrupt departure from their mother's home to their father's, and wondered whether they were adjusting to the primary role that stepmom Barbara played in their care and therapy. Would that explain what felt like a revolt in the making?

Initially, the strategy worked. Without Barbara in the room, the dynamics of the sessions changed – there was less tension and criticism; conversations happened at a slower pace. Kyle and Kayla became more expressive. Kyle opened sessions with his feelings and vigorously complained about the behavior management program. Alex continued to defend the program and to blame Kyle for his lack of cooperation. Underneath, I saw a dad with little confidence in himself, who struggled to express his own emotions. It was difficult for him to be vulnerable. This was a critical realization for me, as I understood that Alex didn't trust himself as a parent anymore. He was scared and overwhelmed, clinging hard to the life preserver of a behavioral management program offered to him by the experts. I understood he needed help and support in reclaiming his power and reconnecting with his children. Processing this in supervision helped me move sessions into processing emotions instead of reports on all that had gone wrong during the week. Over time, as I coaxed and modeled responses for Alex, it became easier for him to acknowledge his children. While it didn't stop escalations at school or at home, I felt more effective in my ability to provide Alex with the tools to check in with himself as he struggled to manage the stress of a demanding full-time job, a wife who resented his lack of involvement, and a program that felt like an intruder.

Reaching Out to Collaborate

As the months went on, I continued to meet with Alex and his two children, as well as he and Barbara as a couple. During this time, Kyle's behavior escalated at school, and Barbara handed the program management over to Alex. I became increasingly frustrated watching this family struggle under an intervention that, in my opinion, was becoming "the enemy." *How could this possibly bring them all closer together? And how much more could the family system take?* Everyone felt they were failing – the parents, children, and me. I felt burdened and frustrated by this behavior program; like being on a sinking ship unable to bail the water out fast enough.

I voiced my opinion in supervision and obtained my supervisor's blessing (there was a politically delicate situation as the children's hospital was affiliated with the center in which I worked) to connect with the case psychologist and share what I witnessed. As a counseling intern, I was low on the food chain. But I was clear in my belief that, because of the work I was doing with this family, I saw them in a way the medical professionals did not. It was my time to protest and to challenge authority. I wanted to know what we were missing, because something was not right.

I took a deep breath and made the call. Polite and professional, I provided an update on my experience of the family and how the behavioral management program was being administered by Alex and Barbara. I contended that adults would be unable to sustain the inspections these two children had to endure – doors taken off their bedrooms; refrigerators being locked to avoid unapproved snacks; isolation from others until behavior was complied with; parents taking time off work to manage children; and charts tracking success and failures. The psychologist was receptive and empathetic. What I described, he said, was not the intent of the program and he agreed that the reins were pulled too tightly. I was intensely relieved. I experienced relief that I'd made the call. Relief that my concerns were validated. Relief that, despite my limited power, I could trust my intuition and judgment to challenge the experts when needed. We agreed that family therapy had an important contribution to make in this family's emotional growth, and my work with them continued.

Shouting from the Rooftop

The longer I worked on this case, the more it felt like an archaeological dig. Every time I turned a corner, something else would pop up. Kyle's behavior continued to escalate and so did the family's. Mutiny was palpable. Something had to give, and it did.

One evening, Kyle climbed out of his bedroom window onto the roof with a knife and threatened to jump. The police were called and, while assessing the situation, Barbara told them she did not feel safe with Kyle in the house. Thus, he was taken to a nearby psychiatric facility where he stayed for several days. While there, Kyle managed to call CPS to report what happened and that he did not want to return to his dad's house. An inquiry was initiated, and it was agreed that he and Kayla would spend a month with their mom and stepdad.

Kyle was nothing if not strategic; determined to be heard even if it meant he had to shout it from the rooftop. I heard him loud and clear. While I wasn't entirely surprised that the system was starting to crack, I understood that the cycle of chaos was intolerable for all involved. There seemed to be little room for the expression of love, compassion, and empathy in this family system. Yet, I was sure that those very expressions of love and empathy were key to unlocking their cycle. It was heartbreaking to witness, which gave me more evidence that I, too, needed to shout − "this isn't working!"

Kyle and Kayla spent most of the summer with their mother and stepdad. CPS called a family meeting of all constituents to review the situation, and I was asked to attend. I was unnerved by having to participate in such an official meeting. I had no idea what would transpire, or what was expected of me, except to report on what I had experienced with the family, if needed. I remember thinking, I'm an intern, what do I know?, as I faced a large conference table of all the people in the case − social worker, caseworker, CPS supervisor, two sets of parents, three sets of grandparents, an uncle, both children, and me. Kyle and Kayla sat at one end of the table with Mary and Glen, who had married the week before. Alex and Barbara sat directly across from me, with their arms around each other, avoiding eye contact with Mary and their children. It was tense and intimidating. I saw a family in pain and felt I needed to advocate for Kyle and Kayla, if given the chance.

After 90 minutes of hearing from all sides, it was decided that Kyle and Kayla would return to their father's house at the end of the summer. The senior CPS supervisor recommended strongly that Alex and his ex-wife, Mary, immediately get on the same page regarding their co-parenting. She predicted that if they did not, they would be back in several years' time to discuss a far more serious situation. I was so relieved. Several times in supervision I had discussed how powerful it could be to get the children's parents into therapy to promote their unity, even though they would not agree to this. However, now I had the authority, through the CPS supervisor, to influence Alex and his ex-wife Mary to attend counseling together so that they could work on co-parenting and creating a common front for the children.

Stabilizing the Hierarchy

Alex and Mary agreed to attend therapy together, and what I saw surprised me. After hearing "stories" about each of them in therapy, I was impressed by how easily they shared their perspective. While initially tense, they agreed it was important to have a communication plan with regular check-ins the children could witness, with common guidelines and boundaries consistently applied in each household. I was relieved: this was a workable dyad! I was excited that this might decrease in-session escalations triggered by stepparents. And, I was hopeful that if Alex and Mary could unite in parenting, the family system could find its way to support two children longing to know they were loved unconditionally.

As Mary and Alex created greater stability through their communication plan, the benefits were visible. Kyle acted out less and reports of escalated behavior reduced. Parents learned to trust their own parenting – a huge shift compared to when I first met with them. With regular consultations and cooperation, each parent became better at co-parenting.

I continued to see Kyle and Kayla while they lived with their mom and stepdad during the summer. While it was not a bed of roses, family members reported that life was quieter, transitions between households went more smoothly, and the children appeared happier. At summer's end, Alex moved to the west coast for a new job and the children remained with Mary and Glen. New schools, and a long-distance relationship with their father, presented new challenges and adjustments. Tension flared between Kyle and his stepdad, which generated new behavior concerns that we processed in our sessions.

After 18 months of working with Kyle, Kayla, and their family, my internship came to an end, and I needed to pass them on to a new intern to continue the work on Kyle's behavior and Kyle and Glen's relationship. Kyle, Kayla, Mary, Glen, and their stepsister, Cassie, attended our last session together. We reviewed all the progress they'd made, some of the challenges that lay ahead, and I expressed my appreciation of our time together. We said our goodbyes and as I wished them the best, Cassie piped up, "Laurie, will you remember us?" In truth, I will never forget all that I learned in our time together and will carry this family's imprint on my heart, always.

Post-Therapy Reflections

The universe brings us clients with lessons to teach – about our profession, about the human experience, and, most importantly, about ourselves. Absolutely, there were days on the drive home I thought I'd never be the kind of therapist these clients needed. I wanted everyone to feel better, but when they were stuck, I felt stuck. I, too, needed a sign that things would get better. I struggled with wanting results quickly – if they could have relief, then so could I. It is not easy to watch clients in pain and conflict; it is uncomfortable and unsettling. And the more complicated the case became, the easier it was to slide the slippery slope of self-doubt and self-judgment – how was I ever going to do this? Some days, the responsibility overwhelmed me.

Here, supervision played an invaluable part in learning patience and staying grounded in the middle of chaos. I looked forward to my weekly supervision as a safe haven to express my doubts, to brainstorm therapeutic strategies, and for guidance. My supervisor's reassurance and validation were soothing. It became my own hour of therapy, not only about my clients, but to process my own unfolding as a therapist. Shedding the mantle of expert I had enjoyed in my former professional life left me feeling vulnerable. I was hard on myself as I watched video sessions with a critical eye, focused on where I got lost or missed something that was said, and wondered at what point I would feel more comfortable in the therapist's chair. With time, I surrendered to the fact that I wasn't going to speed-dial my way through this case or my internship, and appreciated that the "process of becoming" was developmental. Once I understood that, the clock stopped ticking and I felt greater acceptance of both myself and my clients. We were on a journey together where we would all learn, grow, and evolve. It was ok not to be the expert, but, getting to that point took patience with myself, and with my clients.

Staying grounded during chaos with so many players in the field was a challenge. I faced weekly sessions with some trepidation as I anticipated the reports of misbehavior, arguments, and family disagreements. The more I heard, the more I felt swept up in waves of dysfunction and powerlessness. Here, supervision helped me to process my self-of-the-therapist reactions; I learned how to manage the overwhelm, keep the overarching perspective, and to focus on the process rather than the content. It is easy to get caught up in the weeds of a case, but attention to the therapeutic process was, and continues to be, very grounding. "Divine detachment" became my silent mantra in moments of client escalation as I remembered to observe and not absorb!

In my experience, the unfolding of a therapist is a process over time and continues long after an internship is finished. It occurs with every new case and with every new life experience the therapist accumulates. This family provided me with a pivotal experience of self-discovery and growth as a therapist. I carry them with me in gratitude and appreciation, and in hope that I may have made a small difference in their lives.

4

I HAVE A VOICE AND YOU MAY NOT LIKE IT

Courage and Connection in a Psychiatric ER

Karen Kinman

Supervision Issues by Connie S. Cornwell

The professionals that work in mental health are diverse, each governed by their own training and licensing requirements. Sometimes it is not easy to be the new professional entering an established homogenous group. This may be especially true for a family therapist, if the group is focused on the individual patient and their pathology. This can occasionally create a difficult and territorial situation where the professionals cannot find a way to collaborate. This was true for Karen as she was part of a pilot project in which she was the family therapist embedded in a community hospital's psych ER. My challenge, as her supervisor, was to support her in being therapeutic to the whole system while asserting herself as a fellow professional who has value. I supported Karen to reframe and depersonalize the suspicion, anger, and hostility she faced from some of the other professionals as their fear of the unknown, helping her to find compassion. It is easier said than done, but the focus of the relational specialist is on connecting and, hopefully, finding others who are receptive to the systems approach. My main job with Karen was to validate her struggle and to be on call to debrief, as needed. It is not easy to be in an unreceptive system and not catch the disease of judgment, anger, and reactivity. Thus, I listened without judgment, supported and helped her do her work, while not being at the effect of the environment.

But, as a supervisor, how do I practice what I preach and not catch the disease? For me, this has its roots in my spiritual journey, and a core spiritual belief that we are all One. When I find myself reactive and feeling a victim to my circumstances, I draw on that spiritual awareness. I find my connection to the "other," whether person or situation, and realize this reflects me. What do I have to learn here? Perhaps it is as simple as compassion for myself. I am then free to choose how I will react, taking responsibility for my response. It is an internal, ongoing process, often needing time before I reach the freedom I so desire. "In the stillness of Presence, you can sense the formless essence in yourself and in the other as one. Knowing the oneness of yourself and the other is true love, true care, true compassion" (Tolle, 2005, p. 177).

I Have a Voice and You May Not Like It

I was asked to participate in a pilot study incorporating a family therapist into a psychiatric emergency room team. I am very familiar with working in a hospital environment, since I was a nurse for over 30 years, and had practiced in various areas of adult medicine, in addition to pediatric gastroenterology. The majority of my experience has been in the neonatal ICU, where I was a bedside nurse and then an assistant supervisor to an 80-bed unit. I was also a traveling nurse, working in different neonatal units across the country and being exposed to different cultures, populations, and personalities. As a traveler, I had to have the ability to be a fully functioning staff member after a day of orientation. Lastly, I worked as a family care coordinator in a neonatal ICU, evolving the role to include supporting and educating parents and families.

It was my experience in this care coordinator role that gave me the impetus to become a family therapist. From the beginning of my nursing career I examined everything from a holistic lens – mind–body–spirit – and

patients in the context of their families, friends, and worklife. Therefore, I had skills which a new therapist may not have had, including
being trained in hypnotherapy, and being a therapeutic touch practitioner (a healing modality derived from the laying on of hands). My
passion was integrating traditional medicine with complementary
evidence-based therapies for optimal care. And, I was also an advocate
for patients and families, helping them navigate through the healthcare
system. Thus, becoming a family therapist was a midlife career change,
an opportunity to integrate knowledge gained across many professional experiences, and I was looking forward to this new role in the
psych ER.

The Initiation of Integration

My story takes place in a large county hospital which was affiliated
with a medical school. This hospital was undergoing changes in
management, as well as a change in the delivery of care, which
necessitated a significant cultural change. The physician over the psych
ER wanted a more patient-centered, interdisciplinary model of deliver-
ing care that attended to patients' families, which necessitated including
a family therapist as an integral part of the team. He was also hoping to
reduce transfers to psychiatric hospitals. I looked forward to working in
this area of the hospital; I imagined collaborating with the ER team and
bringing a different perspective toward patients' presenting problems.
The department head gave me carte blanche: "Just go and do what you
know how to do!"

Working in the psych ER were social workers, psychiatrists, nurses,
and an addiction counselor. Rotating through the psych ER were
medical students, medical residents, and psychology graduate students.
There were also technicians who stayed with the patients and moni-
tored vital signs, assisted in care, and participated in maintaining safety
for patients and staff. In addition, outside consultants who were observing hospital operations were present, observing all staff and management, and providing input in monthly staff meetings.

I was a bit nervous about working with patients who had schizophrenia and psychosis. My fear in working with severe mental illness
related partly to not knowing how to help, how to be most effective in

alleviating some of their suffering. The depiction of serious mental illness in the media probably contributed to my fears, as well. The required preparation for starting work in the unit, and the actual environment of the psych ER, did not put me at ease. On one day of orientation, I had to learn how to defend myself without harming the patient if he or she grabbed or attacked me. I was told not to wear anything around my neck so I couldn't be strangled, and was taught to keep a certain amount of distance between myself and the patients.

The psych ER was a locked unit. To enter the staff area, which was enclosed in glass and separated from the patients' waiting area, I had to punch in a code to open the door. It reminded me of being in a fishbowl, as I stood in the patients' waiting area looking in on the doctors and nurses. The "fish," in their own environment, were kept safe from the outside world. This outside world, the patients' space, was a large room with a widescreen television. There were vinyl chairs which could extend if patients wanted to sleep, and off the main room were small rooms where the patients would meet with the healthcare team.

My role in the department was to participate in the development of patients' treatment and discharge plans, assess the level of functioning of patients, couples, and families, determine their strengths helpful for recovery, provide immediate couples and family crisis therapy intervention, coordinate with the interdisciplinary team on referral sources and follow-up care, and serve as a liaison with one of the clinics that provided family and couples therapy. My objectives for my first week were to observe staff interactions, the process of delivery of care, the department's structure and hierarchy, and to get comfortable being on the unit.

On my first day, I was introduced to the staff as a family therapist who would attend to patients and their families. It was on this first day that I was told by a senior social worker that I wasn't needed and would be more helpful in other parts of the hospital.

The social workers and other mental health professionals told me they already did patient-centered care, and explained "we do what you do; we know Bowen." I repeatedly worked to reassure staff that I had joined to support and integrate care, not to do what they do. They did not have the time, with all that was included in their job descriptions, to attend to families as well.

Relationships among staff were strained, and the departments that needed to work together most days – the psych ER and main ER – did not have a good working relationship. The staff in the main emergency department often felt unsupported by the psych ER staff when calling for a mental health evaluation for a patient. At the same time, the psych ER staff felt overburdened. I surmised, from my nursing perspective, that the staff in the main ER experienced anxiety around mental illness that went unaddressed. Physicians focused on the disease or diagnosis, nurses knew how to be present and help with grief and loss, but they did not have the training to address severe behavior, suicidal ideation, or other mental illness. A social worker or other mental health professional from the psych ER was always called in.

I can honestly state that this was the *most hostile environment in which I have ever worked*. I did my job under constraints placed on me by the staff and existing policies of the unit. I had permission from the head of the department to see families; however, if anyone needed the room, my work with the patients stopped. I had to leave. Social work tolerated me as I did my own work, but I had interruptions, interference, and really no voice in treatment or discharge plans. So, I became creative. Once I assessed and evaluated, I took a "ready-aim-fire" approach to the issue.

I got practice at one-session meetings with patients, and I found empty rooms outside the ER which staff only occasionally used. I didn't allow my frustrations to interfere with the goal of helping these patients and families. A few meaningful and targeted therapeutic conversations were better than none. I also thought about my experiences with the staff and how I allowed much of their behavior to slide. However, in retrospect, if I had taken the time out to address staff behaviors, I truly don't think I would have changed anything. The system's patterns were so ingrained, and there was no one present who had meaningful authority over staff. While the department head was supportive of me and my role, he was often absent in the unit, and busy with adminis-trative work. The manager position for the social workers changed several times during my work in the ER, and each manager was unable to exert power over the social work staff. Thus, I made a conscious decision to use my energy for patients and families. The patients and families were my priority; the staff, my second.

I know what it's like to feel invisible, and it was eerie. In monthly staff meetings, I sat by myself among a row of empty chairs, no one speaking to me. While in the unit, the staff would pass by me as if I didn't exist. My words dissipated into the air. The social workers had a lot of power in the unit, and there was an unspoken rule that if they thought you were incompetent, you were going to have a difficult time working there. This placed me in a double bind, and I was ignored whether or not I did my job there. So, I made the decision to just let go by completely ignoring this impossible environment. Surrendering to the absurdity of the situation allowed me to disconnect from the negativity and find freedom and a sense of humor.

Strategic Moves within a Problematic System

I do believe you can find good even in the most terrible circumstances, and there were a few gifts that came out of my experience in the ER, one of which was the opportunity to grow my voice. I had something important to contribute. I learned how to be more assertive, and trust in myself and my competency. The themes of not being "good enough" and having my opinions or judgments be perceived as incorrect or inferior and be dismissed, aligned with childhood wounds. In my family-of-origin, my mother was in charge, and even the adults in the family deferred to her. Having different opinions was not allowed. I did not have my own voice, as I learned at an early age that it wasn't safe. I learned that if you did dissent, get angry, or rebel, you were excommunicated from the family; if mom cut off family members, no one else in the family could speak with them either. I knew I would need to wait until I was on my own to begin to develop a voice and explore my own style. I have been told on more than one occasion that I can be too self-critical. Growing my voice has been a gradual process through the years. My experience of being dismissed emerged through-out my professional life, usually by having to take the "one-down position" and working within the medical hierarchy status quo. How-ever, at this point in my life, I knew I was good enough. I was more than good enough. Thus, my sense of not being valued in this position hit at my core; working with the social workers in the psych ER challenged me in this process of growing my voice.

There was one senior social worker who wielded much of the power within the group of social workers with whom I needed to collaborate. Her influence in the social work subsystem mirrored the role my mother played in my family system. She seemed to be in charge, setting the tone in the unit among her peers. Her opinions filtered through to the entire group – if she did not like you, or believed you were inept, other social workers followed suit. One day during rounds, I contributed some information, and a social worker whom I hadn't yet met grimaced and shuddered hearing me talk. Her nonverbal language was blatant: she was not going to acknowledge anything I would bring to the conversation. I continued to be amazed at the behaviors I was confronted with that characterized this system.

During my second week on the unit, I accompanied a team to meet with a 16-year-old girl who came in at midnight with the police. Janie attacked her sister with a knife, and her mother had called 911. She came in handcuffed, fighting with the police officer. Upon admission, there was a crisis meeting with the patient's mother and sister, who both stated that they did not feel safe with the patient at home. They wanted her to go to a psychiatric facility. That morning, the psychiatrist, the senior social worker (who perceived me to be incompetent and thought I would be helpful elsewhere in the hospital), the psychiatry resident, and I walked past the tech who was standing guard outside one of the few rooms for patients who needed greater privacy.

It was 8 am. The psychiatrist woke Janie up and asked how she was feeling. Opening one eye at a time, slowly, Janie replied that she was better and did not want to go to a facility. "I want to go home." The psychiatrist asked her about last night and she replied, "My sister is an idiot." The psychiatrist was done talking with her. She immediately walked out with the rest of the team behind her, looked at me and said, "Why don't you talk with her." The rest of the team then returned to the department and spent the next hour on their computers documenting and making phone calls and arrangements for a transfer, while I stayed behind.

I asked Janie if she wanted to talk and if it was ok for me to sit down. She agreed. I began mapping out her family genogram which she took an interest in. As I was filling in the genogram and gathering information, I did a lot of reframing and pointing out her strengths, as well as strengths within the family unit. Janie had a diagnosis of bipolar disorder and had stopped taking her medications. Her older sister, whom she attacked, moved back into the home four months ago with her 9-month-old son. Curiously, this was also about the time Janie's depression started to increase and the family began having problems with her.

During our time together, Janie was the one who came up with goals and mapped out the steps she needed to take to achieve them. She wanted to have a better relationship with her sister and more time with her mom. I wrote the plan down for her, then had her talk about her new role as an aunt, how important that was, and what that meant to her. This shifted her thinking from how the new baby took her place in the family to giving her a significant and special role only she could fill. Further, she began thinking of future goals for herself, which included going back to school.

Afterward, I approached the team's social worker and told her that I thought Janie could go home, but stated we needed to have another meeting with the family. The social worker said, "We already had a meeting last night and it did not go well, and the family doesn't want her home." I explained about the big change in the family with the patient's sister's new baby and how this coincided with Janie's depression and nonadherence.

The social worker began teaching me, explaining to me why I was wrong. "She will use her anger whenever she wants to manipulate her mother." I explained that I understood what she was saying, but that I work from a different paradigm (*I don't do what you do*). The social worker continued speaking to me as if I were her student, so I knew I needed to be more explicit in my defense. While I knew I had to pick my battles, this was a battle worth fighting, for Janie and her family. Calmly and respectfully, I explained, "I am a doctor. I have a PhD in family therapy, I'm doing postdoc work, and these are my recommendations based on my clinical training and education. I understand the psychiatrist has the ultimate decision." She leaned back in her chair, raised her eyebrows, crossed her arms against her chest, and said, "You're a doctor?" After this conversation, the social worker remained uncommunicative; she did not speak to me, even if we had a mutual patient. When I sat down to a computer next to hers, she got up and moved to a different computer. I thought, *What have I gotten myself into? This system is really dysfunctional.* This behavior continued for weeks until, upon the advice of my supervisor, I apologized to her for arguing.

Unfortunately, I was unable to meet with Janie and her family and address the underlying family interactional patterns and attachment wounds that contributed to the problem. I spoke with the psychiatrist about my session with Janie and my recommendations. However, the psychiatrist was uncomfortable in sending her home because of the initial contact the night before that had gone so poorly.

My interaction with the psychiatrists grew as time went on. As I was getting a lot of practice growing my own voice, I also modeled professional behavior. After a couple of months, the psychiatrists were calling on me for help, and the psychiatrist who saw Janie asked if I would sit down with her and discuss my approach to some of her cases. After two months, one of the social workers also began warming up to me, and would invite me to sit in with her patients or ask me for help.

As a rule, if the team ignored my opinion or recommendation, I went right to the patient and family. I formed coalitions with the patients against a dysfunctional healthcare system which was punitive and pathologizing, while at the same time attempting to support staff. Whenever I said I was going to go back into the waiting area to speak with a patient who was experiencing a psychotic episode, the staff would tell me, "Don't bother, he's psychotic; you won't get any information from him." I had to be a voice for these patients and make the effort to understand, join their world, find their meaning, and connect.

I sat down next to Manuel, a young Latino whom the team evaluated and diagnosed as psychotic. He was waiting to be transferred to a psychiatric facility. He was jumpy, his speech was rapid, and he seemed to have flight of ideas. As I was present with him, a member of the staff came over and asked if I could talk with his family and then send them away. They emphasized that family members had no place in a psych ER, and they were not allowed to receive information on the patient as he was an adult. I asked permission from the patient to talk with them, as they were waiting outside.

I took the family to a room located outside the unit. The patient's mother, sister, and brother (who all lived with him) were present, as well as his aunt; they were very worried. This Latino family did not understand why they could not see Manuel or receive any information. Sitting down, being present, and listening to them de-escalated some of their anxiety. I told them I had a good conversation with Manuel and shared some information. The family was such an important part of his care, and a tremendous resource for me.

Manuel's sister was the one who called the ambulance. She said his behavior began changing more and more as the week went on; he was talking rapidly and describing strange thoughts. She stated that they didn't believe he was psychotic, but the doctor wouldn't listen to them. Manuel was overly concerned with his weight and had begun taking over-the-counter diet pills about two weeks ago. I asked if he was taking any other medication, and his sister stated, "Oh, yes, he takes something for a medical condition he has had for years." The combination of these medications certainly could have caused the patient's erratic behavior and speech.

I went back to the psychiatrist who had evaluated Manuel and told him he had begun taking diet pills two weeks ago, in addition to his prescription medication. With this information, the psychiatrist completely changed the diagnosis, which altered the course of treatment. The patient's sister called me a few weeks after her brother came home to tell me how thankful and incredibly grateful they were for my help.

One session I had with Liza, a woman who came in needing help with addiction, was a mirror image of a therapeutic conversation that I, myself, needed. A few staff members were looking at the patient's chart on the computer and I heard them laughing because she had a degree in English. Of course, I was curious, and went out into the patient waiting area to find her. She had mascara smeared down her cheeks because she'd been crying, and was sitting in the chair with her head down, in a fetal position. I asked if she wanted to talk while she waited, and she nodded. We went into one of the small rooms.

Both of Liza's parents were physicians, and she was the artistic one in the family. The messages she got from her parents and others were that she needed to stop wasting her time and do something to support herself financially so she could live a more comfortable lifestyle. She was brilliant and creative. She was happy when she was surrounded by her artistic and creative peers, with whom she could collaborate, and at these times she didn't need alcohol or drugs. By the end of the session, she looked at me and said, "I get it." She knew what gave her meaning in life and she needed to be true to herself. The talents she had were not valued by those around her.

Reflections on the Process

After the pilot program ended, I made a chart of patients and families I saw with pertinent information, including my interventions and the outcomes. Seeing this on paper, I was proud of myself. I had accomplished quite a bit by myself, despite the adversity and resistance. Even when some of the outcomes were not optimal, I did my best to bring my assessments and evaluations to the team. I *did* matter, and was doing work that had tremendous value. My way of thinking, my actions, and my presence made a difference.

Aside from growing my voice, the second gift I was given was the opportunity to work with people living with schizophrenia and severe mental illness. When I focused on the person first, and worked to find what was meaningful to them, and how they experienced their diagnosis and the world around them, I experienced empathy, and discovered patients' creativity, resilience, and strength.

In the psych ER, there was no sense of connection or trust among staff, nor between staff and the patients who came through the doors. This disconnection influenced the quality of the care tasks that needed to be done. Duties were performed without enjoyment; there was no meaningful purpose to the work. In the larger hospital system, administration was facing many stressful changes, with position vacancies and a great deal of turnover in management amid an investigation of fraud by the state. The stakes were high, as there were financial consequences to the hospital if process revisions were not made. The intense stressors that upper-level management were experiencing filtered down to staff on the unit.

In contrast, it was connection that brought me the second gift from this experience. My hesitancy of working with those who live with schizophrenia and severe mental illness disappeared when I was present and engaged. When I refer to connection, it is from the perspective of a therapeutic touch practitioner. Therapeutic touch, as a modality, operates from the premise that all human beings are open systems and have a constant energy exchange with others and the environment. There are three essential ingredients that must be present: you must have a sincere intent to help or heal, you must be centered and focused, and you must work on self-introspection, focused on your goals of becoming a healer, doing so nonjudgmentally and with acceptance.

Therapeutic touch has allowed me, in a healer role as nurse or therapist, to have deeper connections with others. It is, first, a deep connection with your sincere intent and commitment to relieve pain or suffering in others. As a healer, you are a channel for universal healing energy (love, Holy Spirit, divine light) to mend and repair. Further, a centered state — a state of mindfulness, being in the present, a trance-like state of focused attention — is a necessary ingredient for the healer in their practice of therapeutic touch. The goal is to help the patient or client achieve centeredness and balance. And you, as healer, also become more integrated in the process. I use therapeutic touch as a healing modality in therapy for clients experiencing trauma, depression, anxiety; it also helps me, as I center myself prior to a session, to connect on a deeper level.

Having practiced therapeutic touch for over 30 years, I can center myself amid the chaos and disorganization around me; I centered myself before entering the unit and sent healing energy to staff and patients. Sometimes I think the process allows me to "get out of the way" — it's not about me, what I think or need — it's about connecting with someone and providing a safe and sacred space to allow that person to do their own work. It is in that space where healing begins.

When I was curious about what a purposeful and meaningful life meant to these patients, and saw them as human beings living with this experience of being schizophrenic, I found them receptive and even grateful for my presence, and I was grateful for them. Having someone sit with them and listen was a rarity, and these patients would thank me for just listening. Even if they were experiencing a psychotic episode, not all that may have appeared as "gibberish" was actually so. I found a great deal of intelligence.

Sometimes, the patients had more insight into the staff than the staff had of them. One morning I walked into the patient waiting area and a man looked up from his blanket to say, "Who are you? You don't work here. You're not like any of them." Another patient with a diagnosis of bipolar disorder saw my poetry book, and we began talking. He told me, as he smiled and pointed at the staff area, that he knows what to do, and what to say to them, to get what he wants.

Prior to this experience, I enjoyed an occasional poem every now and then. I had my favorite poems and authors, but did not appreciate poetry as I do now. This was the third gift I received: I found poems that touched the heart, and discovered poetry could connect quicker and on a deeper level than a conversation. Patients interpreted their own meanings and received healing messages. Poetry speaks to pain and suffering. Poetry speaks to core emotions universal to all. I found poems which spoke to my heart and, suddenly, I wasn't alone. The following poem I wrote speaks to this:

> I have a voice, you may or may not like it.
> The pitch may be too high, or low;
> The pace, too fast or slow.
> Pay less attention with your head
> And listen with your heart.
> You may find what connects us.
> And then, the healing will start.

I would not trade my experience with these patients and their families for anything. I became good at connecting, and finding commonality, purpose, and meaning. However, it was difficult to let go of the day after leaving the unit. I often had to debrief with my supervisor. I exercised and meditated and prayed. I had the support of a group of family therapists who I could rely on. I needed to debrief and talk for many months after my time ended there, as the overall interaction with the staff was traumatic.

My work as a medical family therapist did not end at the psych ER, as I was then assigned to a neurology clinic which focused on patients living with amyotrophic lateral sclerosis (ALS). This clinic was one that truly practiced collaborative care among a multidisciplinary team.

Everyone respected and expected one another's input at the staff meetings when we discussed the patients and their personal issues. We each called upon one another if we needed help or information. The physicians did not hesitate to ask me for help, especially when they believed the patient would benefit from my assistance as a medical family therapist. As a result, it was a place where I felt relaxed, valued, and part of the team. This filtered through to the patients who truly received optimal care.

One morning, a physician came over to me and told me she needed help with an elderly couple in room two. The physician's level of anxiety was high, and she was appropriately concerned. She explained to me that she had stopped her assessment when the caregiver said she felt like killing herself. "I told them you would be coming in to talk with them." I went into the room and talked with the couple, and their older daughter who had come with them to the appointment. This was a complex case with other medical concerns besides ALS, in addition to social and economic concerns. I spoke with the family for a while, then went out to find their physician. I told the physician what my assessment and evaluation was, and that I was not concerned the caregiver would commit suicide, just that she needed a safe place to air her feelings. I also told her I would follow up with the family in a few days. I then spoke with the clinic's social worker, sharing critical patient information and my overall evaluation, as she would be seeing them shortly as well. The team trusted my assessment, and this physician no longer had anxiety about the patient's caregiver.

My co-workers' collaboration gave me the feeling of being valued, especially as the referring physician made a difference in the family's response to me. It was made evident that I was competent, there to be helpful to patients (and their providers), and that I was part of the team. The family viewed me as a contributor with worth, and understood the importance of the role of family therapy in the medical setting.

In sum, this clinic was a wonderful environment. The physicians' visible support for family therapists in their clinic influenced everyone's perception of me and my profession. More broadly, the physicians respected and valued the staff members, and each of the staff members respected, valued, and relied on each other's knowledge and experience.

Upper management was integrated in the clinic, and the respect flowed downward from the top. I missed the clinic when I left; I missed the work and I missed the people.

These varied experiences – both positive and negative, welcoming and not – have influenced me both as a person and a therapist. For quite a while after graduating, and through my internship, I attempted and reattempted to "fit" into a healthcare system that is not working and, in my opinion, creates more patients and disempowers. I have since made the decision to be true to myself, and have developed a private practice. This practice has evolved from a traditional family therapy practice to an integrative, holistic mental health practice. I help clients facilitate their connection with mind–body–spirit for whatever levels of healing they seek. Each of us has unique lessons we must learn, as well as the universal process of learning how to love ourselves and one another. From these experiences, I know, more so now, that my voice, my perspectives, and my skills are needed and can make a great deal of difference. I also know that all that I offer is not good for everyone, but I am here, present, and willing when someone comes to me for help. I have a voice, and you may not like it, but that's ok. I have found others who do.

Part II Conclusion

The clients described in Part II all presented powerful experiences with larger systems for the therapists-in-training. While Chapter 3's family required the therapist to collaborate with external systems who were at times pathologizing and themselves trapped in the family's chaos, Chapter 4 describes an intensely problematic work environment that actively spurned the family therapist and her work. Key for both was the safe haven that supervision provided, in order to meaningfully reflect on the therapists' interactions with these other providers, and what it meant for the competence they felt as interns. Both of these chapter authors were also second career therapists, with experiences of developing their confidence many times over. They artfully demonstrate the delicate, at times thorny, nature of collaboration, while providing compelling examples of how to prioritize clients' well-being and maintain personal conviction and assuredness. Though both women describe questioning their own competence, the certainty with which they stand in their power, claim their authority, and serve their clients, provides important models for therapists struggling with wavering confidence.

In addition to providing valuable examples of teamwork, these stories also emphasize the importance of remaining immune to the disease. In other words, preventing oneself from falling prey to a highly contagious, individualizing, problem-centered narrative is key to promoting healing. Further, preserving one's own practices of healing and self-care can emphasize for therapists their self-worth, and provide sustaining energy to combat toxic larger systems. Many experiences of inter-system collaboration are rich opportunities for multidisciplinary cross-pollination and serving clients from multiple angles. It is vital for new therapists to develop the skills to grow cooperative relationships, as well as to recognize when their self-of-the-therapist reactions to larger systems are sending them important signals that should not be ignored. Supervision can assist in both of these domains.

Thought Questions

1. Do you assess the influence other professionals and systems have on your cases? What does/could this look like in order to be most meaningful?

2. Have other professionals challenged your systems perspective? How did you handle this challenge? How do you describe the work you do as a couple and family therapist to non-family therapists?

3. What is the difference that makes the difference in our profession compared to other mental health professions? How would you describe the difference?

4. When reading these chapters, where were you finding yourself most reactive? Why is that? Are their overlaps to your own personal or professional experiences?

5. How do these therapists' themes of self-doubt and courage reflect your own growth experiences? How might they inspire you to further growth?

6. How can therapists balance advocating for their clients and families with protecting themselves in systems that do not respect the therapist? What are our ethical obligations, specific to advocacy and promoting healing, in these environments?

7. What are the reframes you found to be most powerful in these chapters? How might you apply that type of thinking in your own work with powerless patients or large systems?

Part III

MEETING MYSELF IN THE ROOM

Introduction to Part III

The therapist's goal and the client's may not be the same. Interns must meet their clients where they are and learn to trust the outcome, even though it may not be what the therapist wanted for the family. This becomes especially challenging when the case intersects with the therapist's own story. We often meet ourselves in the therapy room; as humans, we have much in common. Preparing for, and rising to, the occasions when we find powerful overlaps between the personal and professional is a critically important part of supervision. Supervisors can serve as mirrors, reflecting supervisees' blind spots, internal reactions, and strengths, as well as highlighting isomorphic patterns replicating within and between systems.

Self-of-the-Therapist Work

Self-of-the-therapist work is defined as "the willingness of a therapist or supervisor to participate in a process that requires introspective work on issues in his or her own life, that has an impact on the process of therapy in both positive and negative ways" (Timm & Blow, 1999, p. 333). This work should be predicated on trust and safety in the supervision relationship. First, supervisors should state, up front, that a focus on self-of-the-therapist development is a part of their philosophy of supervision, and that it is a process the supervisor will intentionally emphasize in their work. Thus, supervisors can model an informed consent process, and obtain supervisees' permission to proceed with the supervisory relationship as outlined. Once supervisees are fully informed consumers, the supervisee should be the driver of the self-of-the-therapist learning process, such that they should be able to determine their own goals for exploring personal experiences (Timm & Blow, 1999).

Further, in group settings, supervisors should clearly specify, and repeatedly state, expectations of privacy, sometimes referred to as the "Vegas rule" – what is shared in group supervision, stays in group supervision. Given ethical expectations, and often legal guidelines, that define the supervisory relationship as necessarily confidential, supervisors should also strictly avoid divulging supervisees' confidences shared in dyadic supervision, in larger group settings. Though there may be nuances to the confidentiality of supervision, for example, in order to allow supervisors in learning systems to collaborate in support of trainees, supervisors should still be cautious, guarded, and selective about sharing the specific content of supervisees' self-of-the-therapist work with colleagues. Asking whether sharing the information can meaningfully shape other trainers' work with the supervisee, and whether the supervisee, themselves, cannot otherwise be encouraged to share the information with these supervisors directly, can be important guiding questions.

In addition, emphasizing supervisees' strengths and utilizing a solution-oriented approach to supervision can be especially helpful. In other words, often an emphasis on self-of-the-therapist "issues" includes a negative intonation – what we are looking to process are problems, deficits, and traumas. Instead, searching supervisees' histories and close relationships for assets and skills can provide balance to the work and powerfully inform trainees' applications of themselves in the therapy room. Further, this supervisory stance models for therapists how to be consistently listening for clients' "ladders" – resources they unknowingly carry that may enable them to pull themselves out of their problem-saturated hole.

The role of the supervisor as a mentor necessarily involves an emphasis on the personal development of supervisees as professional family therapists (Morgan & Sprenkle, 2007). This includes the duty of supervisors to assist their learners in developing awareness of their own strengths and areas of growth, processing self-of-the-therapist reactions, and accessing their own mental health support, as needed. As clients are not aware of their strengths, so too may therapists need a boost. As Satir emphasized, therapists who are more aware of their abilities experience growth in their self-esteem and become more able to facilitate healing with clients (Lum, 2002). Moreover, failing to do the important work of processing self-of-the-therapist issues can be problematic in the therapy room. Identifying potential pitfalls and assets is immensely helpful preparation for practice. However, outlining the specific process by which self-of-the-therapist work is done in supervision is critically important to facilitate a safe and productive learning environment for trainees.

Person-of-the-Therapist Model

One such specific approach to self-of-the-therapist work in training is the person-of-the-therapist (POTT) model, developed by Harry Aponte (1982). This model is grounded in the belief that "the vehicle for therapeutic change is a social relationship" between the client and their therapist, therefore leading to unique healing processes in each specific case (Aponte, 2016; Aponte & Winter, 2000, p. 127). Therapists' feelings and reactions that occur with individual families are tools to both understand and shift the system. Thus, the model's proponents contend it is critical to develop therapists' skills in how to use themselves therapeutically (Aponte & Kissil, 2014).

The POTT model emphasizes four intersecting skills for the development of the therapist's personhood, including competence in theoretical skills (i.e., models and frameworks), external skills (i.e., therapeutic techniques), internal skills (i.e., integration of life experience and clinical training), and collaborative skills (i.e., ability to work together with external systems and other professionals on clients' behalves)

(Aponte & Winter, 2000). Further, this approach emphasizes principal emotional issues for therapists and the need to identify and work through these core *signature themes* (i.e., patterns of feeling, thinking, or relating, betrayed by therapists' greatest anxieties, hidden fears, or problematic coping styles) that are pervasive in influencing our internal processes. POTT training centralizes signature theme work in family therapy education, emphasizing "mastering the signature theme in all aspects of the therapeutic process" (Aponte & Kissil, 2014, p. 154). Thus, the POTT model first focuses on growing therapists' self-awareness (via their signature theme, personal history, and worldview). The goal is to support therapists-in-training to grow in their ability to accept, and learn from, their own weaknesses and vulnerabilities (Aponte & Winter, 2000). Second, POTT-oriented supervisors emphasize supervisees' development toward attending and tuning in to their internal reactions within the therapy process. The third and final goal of this training model is to support therapists' abilities to intentionally use their selves in each phase of therapy – joining, observing, evaluating, intervening (Aponte & Kissil, 2014).

Though we move on to highlight specific emphases on the use of self within select family therapy models, the POTT training approach may be overlaid on any theoretical orientation (e.g., Chapter 5 highlights the simultaneous use of Emotionally Focused Couple Therapy [Johnson, 2005] and POTT-specific work on the trainee's signature theme). The process is, instead, focused on developing therapists' self-reflective abilities and their meaningful and intentional use of self in the therapeutic space.

Use of Self and Family Therapy Models

Though the field of marriage and family therapy has approached understanding what makes therapy effective through either a common factors lens (Sprenkle & Blow, 2004) or model-specific theorizing, the self-of-the-therapist is a uniting concept, discussed with significance by proponents of both (Simon, 2006). In other words, several specific family therapy models deal explicitly with the use of the therapist's self in the room, and theorize about the impact of the therapist's personhood on therapeutic effectiveness. Similarly, leaders of the common factors movement have postulated that the self-of-the-therapist is a critical component of therapy, regardless of theoretical orientation. Virginia Satir, (2000) agreed, stating "[The] involvement of the therapist's 'self,' or 'personhood,' occurs regardless of, and in addition to, the treatment philosophy or the approach" (p. 19). As evidence, Blow and Sprenkle (2001) identified that therapist self-awareness and authenticity, among other therapist factors, are common across family therapy models, and likely critical in conveying a positive effect for clients.

Bowen Family Systems Therapy

Bowen's family systems therapy approach directly theorized about the importance of therapists' self-of-the-therapist work. Bowen envisioned the personal development of therapists, and their understanding of their own family-of-origin processes, as integral for therapeutic effectiveness (Kerr & Bowen, 1988). Specifically, this model emphasizes the therapist's differentiation of self, achieved through exploring and directly confronting past emotional processes in the therapist's family-of-origin, as necessary for the effective application of the model's therapeutic techniques. Differentiation – the balanced need for autonomy and connection – protects the therapist from being caught up in a family's process of anxiety and triangulation. The overarching goal of facilitating awareness of systemic emotional processes, and decreasing emotional reactivity, requires a therapist who has this self-awareness and can respond nonreactively. Therefore, training and supervision will emphasize new therapists' levels of differentiation, not specific Bowenian interventions (Brown, 1999).

Importantly, critiques of Bowen's model speak to the types of selves most reflected in the approach's constructs. Namely, greater levels of differentiation reflect a greater tendency toward individuality (Kerr & Bowen, 1988); however, the model provides little explanation of how families (or their therapists) should enhance togetherness. Moreover, this emphasis on the individual and intellectuality reflects the socialization of men and fails to theorize about the worth of emotion-derived knowledge, a particular resource for women (Knudson-Martin, 1994). Thus, as Knudson-Martin (1994) specifies, "because women develop in the context of their relationships, female differentiation involves learning to hear and trust one's own voice at the same time one attends to the voices of others" (p. 40). In considering therapist's use of self, this expanded conceptualization of Bowenian theory may be especially relevant for female therapists-in-training, who may be uniquely in need of growing their confidence, while learning to be fully present in their relationships and with their clients.

Lastly, supervisors may wish to use genograms with their supervisees to map the learner in the context of their family-of-origin, informed by Bowenian theory. While this is a common assignment in family therapy training programs, it may not be an activity that is specifically drawn into the more intimate dyadic supervision relationship. However, this may be especially effective as overlaps between clients' and therapists' genograms can be specifically highlighted (Braverman, 1997). More-over, learning supervisees' family-of-origin processes can assist super-visors in navigating surprising or confusing supervisee reactions to clients, as well as highlight strengths, skills, and resources that the learner has at their disposal, for application in the therapy room (e.g., as in Chapter 2, where the author's supervisor highlights how his experiences juggling parenthood are an asset to his development as a therapist).

Experiential Family Therapy

Another early example of a family therapy approach that specifically and enthusiastically advocated for the importance of therapists' use of self is the experiential model (or symbolic-experiential; Connell, Mitten, & Whitaker, 1993). As the approach is based in the assumption that people can change the most via lived experience, experiential therapists emphasize the therapeutic alliance and their active involvement in the work of therapy. Whitaker (1973, 1989) emphasized that the person-of-the-therapist was, specifically, the most important healing agent of therapy. The use of the therapist's self in the therapy is to reshape and promote healing emotional experiences and influence families' change. Whitaker also defined anxiety as a curative factor, intentionally spreading it across family members and increasing it to help unstick families. For example, experiential therapists may confront families with differences between their emotional experiences and the therapist's experience, which help to activate the system's stress (Mitten & Connell, 2004). Whitaker used his own experiences of anxiety to inform his therapeutic process, specifically enacted aspects of the family's symbolic world, and believed therapeutic impasses were a consequence of a therapist's lack of capacity to tolerate anxiety (Connell et al., 1993; Mitten & Connell, 2004; Whitaker & Malone, 1953).

Satir (2000) expanded these ideas in her *humanistic experiential approach* and emphasized the importance of power in the therapeutic relationship. Specifically, she identified that power dynamics in therapy may serve either the therapist's attempt to control the client or serve to empower the client and foster their agency. Satir clarified that the therapist's use of power, in one regard or the other, is a function of their self-worth and how they manage their own internal needs. If a therapist is lost in their own growth process and unaware of their self-of-the-therapist reactions, she posited they are likely to inappropriately, and unethically, use the therapeutic process for their own gain, to clients' detriment. Conversely, Satir emphasized the therapist's ability to use their personhood for clinical gains; to engage with clients humanely, build the therapeutic alliance, and model vulnerability and change. The positive use of self requires attuning to one's own needs, exploring one's own life experiences, self-care, and therapeutic competence (Satir & Baldwin, 1983). Satir argued that the process of achieving personal congruence, and being fully connected and present with oneself, benefits the therapist as a person as well as their therapeutic process (Satir, Banmen, Gerber, & Gomori, 1991). Similarly, supervisors using Satir's model should also work to achieve their own personal congruence, in order to best assist their supervisees in processing their self-of-the-therapist experiences (Lum, 2002).

At their core, experiential approaches emphasize the self-of-the-therapist as the most crucial instrument in the therapy process. As such, early theorists were reticent to operationalize much of their assumptions, with concerns that specification locks up the therapist's self and their spontaneity (Keith, 2000). The overarching goal of providing corrective emotional experience is best achieved through therapists' attunement to families' processes and their ability to dance in and out of systems to enact change. This process requires maturity, a great deal of self-of-the-therapist work in training and supervision, and the intentional examination of interpersonal connections between the therapist's self and other selves (e.g., colleagues, clients; Keith, 2000).

In sum, the self-of-the-therapist is an important component of many family therapy models. Choosing among them, however, can be an emphasis of new therapists – there is sometimes comfort and assuredness in knowing the toolbox one is carrying into the room. In choosing a theoretical approach for clinical practice, Simon (2006) advocates that family therapy trainers should recognize, and emphasize, therapists' own contextually constructed worldviews, as well as how these worldviews match with the underlying worldview of their chosen family therapy model. The author postulates, "therapist worldview/model worldview congruence produces a synergistic effect between those elements in the model that contribute to therapeutic efficacy and the therapist factors that contribute to efficacy" (p. 336). Thus, supervisor guidance in highlighting major models' philosophical worldviews and assisting supervisees to process how their own life experiences may inform their case conceptualization, model choice, and clinical practice, is a critical component of emphasizing worldview congruence.

Fears of Incompetence: It's Totally Normal

As each of the chapters in Part III highlights, new therapists' fears of incompetence are commonplace (Patterson, Williams, Edwards, Chamow, & Grauf-Grounds, 2018). Feeling uncertain and self-critical are regular experiences for individuals new to the field (Frediani & Rober, 2016). But, as these fears are insidious they can develop gradually, sneak out and surprise, or entrap new therapists from any angle. High levels of anxiety can impact trainees' focus, memory, and presence in session (Rønnestad & Skovholt, 2003). Further, this type of fear is isolating – new therapists commonly believe they are alone in their limitations and anxiety, and may even hide these concerns from safe supervisors. Thus, it is necessary for supervisors to create an open, trusting supervision environment (Anderson, Schlossberg, & Rigazio-DiGilio, 2000), but perhaps not sufficient for identifying and addressing imposter syndrome. Supervisors should therefore be intentional about normalizing insecurities and validating supervisees when they share these anxieties.

Therapists' concerns that they are incapable of providing quality care for a family show up particularly when presenting problems loom large and are seductive in their details. Trainees can quickly get sucked into the content of a session, rather than emphasizing the process. Shifting supervisees' attention back to systemic operations and relational dynamics is a continual part of supervision. In addition, supervisors can highlight the isomorphism between families being lost in their own problem-saturated narratives, defining and pathologizing one another using narrowly defined, content-driven parameters, and the therapist's similar process. Trainees' self-of-the-therapist work, outside of their clinical practice, can help to free the therapist from becoming entrenched in clients' content. In part, this process can access strengths the learner has at their disposal – crowbars to extricate themselves out of their own reactivity and fears of inadequacy, as described above. Additionally, experiencing intervention success can quickly counter a therapist's lack of confidence, even though extreme fluctuations in anxiety are typical for new supervisees (Bischoff, Barton, Thober, & Hawley, 2002).

Though we discuss in the introduction to Part II the potential to use a "fake it 'til you make it" approach to building confidence, this is not preferable if a therapist has, in fact, reached the limits of their competence. It is critically important that supervisees are able to pragmatically assess their skill sets and developmental needs, and bring these to supervision. While perfectionism may be an issue for new therapists, and one that supervisors should highlight and confront (Patterson et al., 2018), supervisors and supervisees both carry an ethical responsibility to identify realistic competency boundaries and additional training needs. These can be challenging to tease out at the early stages of therapists' development, as much is new and their anxieties may get in the way. Supervision may therefore benefit from the transparent use of specific practice-based competencies, and regular self-evaluation and supervisory feedback to assess learners' growth over time.

Honoring Clients' Autonomy

A final way we, the therapists, may show up in the therapy room is in our own, personal goals for our clients. As we connect with clients, and they become part of our lives, we may begin to emphasize what we think they *should* be doing, rather than what is best for them. This process may reflect the notion of *willfulness*, or the process of denying reality, trying to fix what is out of our control, refusing to shift gears when needed, or giving up (Linehan, 2015; May, 1982). However, the outcomes we think clients should achieve are not always what they end up with. Supervisees should be encouraged to listen to where families are and more clearly to what they need. Therapists must honor what clients wish for and let go of their own agenda. The ability to detach from clients' outcomes may be especially difficult when their presentation intersects with our own self-of-the-therapist issues. In these spaces, respecting clients' autonomy and reminding ourselves that we are only a small part of anyone's life journey is important.

5

ONE VOICE AMONG MANY
The Goal of Therapy Belongs to the Clients

Mindy Howard

Supervision Issues by Connie S. Cornwell

Competence is always an issue for early career therapists. How does one instill this quality when beginning interns want so much the approval of their supervisor and clients? The need to be liked is strong; however, one learns that having clients like you is not enough to create change and move clients toward their goals. Wavering confidence does not stop with the intern therapist; the supervisor can also question her own competency. *Can I help grow this therapist? Do I have the tools, the right approach, and the necessary understanding to help this person become an effective clinician?*

After one has been a therapist for a while, you realize times of seeming failure offer the most opportunity for growth as a professional. I realize I could redo every session I have ever done. Hindsight offers growth in our profession and as we are process therapists we do self-correct along the way. As a supervisor, I reveal my vulnerability as a nonexpert and share the struggles and challenges

I have faced in therapy to balance being seen as the "expert," as well as the myth that I have the power to solve problems. As supervisors we can demonstrate to our interns that change is in the system – the clients have the power to change and, at best, we become adept at facilitating it. It is a collaboration.

Even though therapy is goal-directed, it is best not to be tied to the result, as then it becomes more about me, the therapist, rather than meeting the clients where they are and respecting their knowingness. Often the result is something different than the one we hoped for, as with Mindy's second case, and we must accept the clients' ending. Mindy was hopeful the couple and their son and daughter-in-law would come together, reconnect, and form a bond. Although the goal was partially met, it was not the ultimate reunion Mindy was striving to achieve. Mindy learned how clients can surprise us with a different conclusion. She learned she is just a small part of the clients' journey, which continues beyond therapy, and she came to the realization that her work with this family was beneficial.

One Voice among Many

I joined the field of family therapy later in life, after a season of raising children, teaching yoga, supporting my husband through medical school, and establishing his practice. My oldest kids were finishing high school when I finally started my training. I met the clients described herein when I was in my early forties and I was a family therapy intern. The clinic where I was training was embedded in a large medical school; referrals came from within the school, as well as from the community. Some clients found us because we operated on a sliding fee scale, reflected in the first couple described. Others came specifically for medical family therapy, as represented in the second couple.

Couple #1: Introductions and Initiating Therapy

The gregarious, fast-talking businessman at the window made a joke about the credit card machine malfunctioning and getting a free session, a stark contrast to the angry lady sitting across the lobby. Perfectly coiffed and striking, she glared at him, and I privately wondered about the implications of asking for discounts on couple therapy when one is already "in the doghouse." He brought her in to repair their eight-year relationship after his infidelity with multiple partners. She discovered one affair by reading his text messages; several partners materialized as she followed the technology trail.

On first impression, he seemed open and easy to talk to, while she seemed distant and hard to read. He shared a sad story about a moment two years prior when he knew they were in trouble. They were having sex and he looked up to see her bored expression, and she was tapping her fingers as if to say, "Are you done yet?" In a vulnerable moment, he was injured and enraged. When the opportunity presented itself, he wanted to be with someone who desired him. He confessed to being sloppy with the last affair, even wanting her to find out because he knew it would hurt. I wanted to get to what led up to that moment in the relationship. He said she's always been cold and unaffectionate. I wondered how these opposites ended up together.

They met online. He was a persistent pursuer in a three-year court-ship where she minimally responded to his attempts and he "wore her down over time." The eldest of five, accustomed to success with women, oozing Spanish machismo, he said he found her challenging.

An only child, she emigrated from Puerto Rico at the age of 11, raised by grandparents when her parents sporadically left the country for months or years at a time. Her protective grandparents rarely allowed her to go out for any reason besides school. With few friends, she grew accustomed to loneliness. She felt affirmed (but sometimes smothered) by his attention.

During our intake session, I felt uneasy when I learned the couple wasn't married. Lots of cases made me uneasy in the beginning, and I was learning this was a sign to pay attention and stay curious. I had only been a family therapy intern for a couple of months. *Could I help an unmarried couple save their relationship with such traumatic attachment wounds?* I wondered about why they never married. I wondered what kept them from calling it quits. I felt limited; my inexperience with unmarried partnerships would require some supervision and inquiry, not knowing much about what keeps couples together when they have chosen not to marry. I have been married for 19 years; I could remember a few occasions when the vows I took were the only thing standing between me and the door, and the same was true for my husband. How do unmarried partners navigate these periods when one or both want to flee? What keeps them fighting for the relationship? How is an unmarried bond different or the same as a married one?

I gave them a few exit ramps during the first session. Before I met with this couple, I had experienced a difficult session with another couple where I had not adequately prepared for couple therapy. They were a family therapy client; the parents were triangulating their adult daughter to diffuse tension in the couple relationship. When we met for our first couple session, I was not experienced enough to slow down their ferocious reactive cycle. They brought their painful stories and, without the ability to help de-escalate them, I lost them as a client. The wife's angry demeanor felt so threatening to me as a new therapist, and I did not get a second chance to continue the work.

Not wanting to repeat that experience, I told them couple therapy could be long and even painful work. I told them it might get worse before it gets better. I told them I would need a commitment from them both that they were "all in" for the long haul. I wanted to give them a frank overview of the process, so they could decide to bail out early if their motivation for therapy was low. They both said they wanted to try as they couldn't envision living apart and they were miserable. When I couldn't give them any more reasons to leave and never come back, we agreed to meet again. I had mixed feelings about delving into a case with another couple after losing my previous client, wanted a chance to try again, but was fearful about whether my skills would be enough for them.

The Therapeutic Process

This couple became my teacher. I immersed myself in Emotionally Focused Couple Therapy (EFT; Johnson, 2005). I read and reread sections of Johnson's manual. I listened to her books on my long drives to work. I watched every EFT session I could get my hands on. I borrowed conference materials on early EFT sessions, mapping conflict cycles, creating enactments.

I was working hard at being their couple therapist, and I had a nagging feeling I may have been working harder than they were. During one memorable session, I observed their reactive conflict cycle for a grueling 80 minutes before getting them to slow down and turn toward each other (note: our sessions are 50 minutes long). It was hard-won, but there was a glimmer of hope at the end of that mess. They looked at one another through tears. Underneath the anger, bitterness, and resentment, she feared being made a fool. He was afraid of failing. She was terrified of being alone. He was afraid of losing the most constant relationship he'd ever had. She was afraid she would never be enough for him. We ploughed on, session after session, mapping the cycle, softening, re-engaging.

When they got reactive, I panicked despite my efforts to stay calm. They got reactive a lot. Their angry dance continued to show up during sessions, and I often lacked the confidence to step in and stop them. This touched on something deep within me that bears reflection.

Fear of Incompetence: A Signature Theme

While I was working on this case, my graduate coursework required me to use Aponte's person-of-the therapist training model to conceptualize my growth as a therapist. We developed our signature theme, "a psychological issue that is at the core of our human woundedness, coloring our emotional functioning throughout our lives" (Aponte & Kissil, 2014, p. 154). According to this model, developing therapists work through this theme and use it to effectively care for clients.

Mine began with a fear of being unimportant, rooted in feelings of incompetence. Memories of the panic I felt as a child when others expected me to perform without enough preparation or training resurfaced, as I found myself as an intern in new situations with clients. I felt exposed, dreading the moment others would see my shame and know that I was a fraud, that I really had no ability to help them. However, while the 7-year-old version of myself was dismissed for choking under pressure, the response from colleagues and supervisors was compassionate as I shared how it feels to not know what to do with clients, and risk letting them down.

Sitting with this couple, no matter how well I knew my theoretical model, no matter how carefully I had planned the structure of the session, I felt incompetent. When they got caught in their reactive cycle (and what passionate fighters they were!) I would freeze up. The arrows kept coming. He stayed out all night. She wouldn't "shut up about the affairs." He changed his passwords. She picked fights. He withdrew. She withdrew but went on the attack when she could no longer tolerate the silence. She preferred a fight to being ignored. He grew weary of her suspicion. Soon pictures of him surfaced at a work conference with other women, along with new messages from one of the mistresses he claimed to have blocked. It was a difficult, tenacious cycle to interrupt.

I also reflected on the shame I felt when I craved the approval of my clients. I believed I should be an island, sturdy and untouched by the opinions of others, secure on my own two feet. However, I desperately wanted to be an effective therapist, doing meaningful work. I wanted to be good at my job. If I wasn't a good enough therapist, was I responsible for the demise of their relationship?

Over the course of that semester, I worked to better understand this desire for the approval of my clients. As systemic therapists, it makes sense that we care deeply about how we are perceived, if we evaluate ourselves based on the experiences and opinions of others. My identity is connected to my competence; if others see me as a valuable member of the community, it affects how I see myself. With time, I accepted that while their opinions mattered to me, they were one voice among many, including my own. As my confidence grew with other cases, I was able to loosen my grip on wanting their approval.

Another layer of my signature theme was how I coped with fears of incompetence by projecting confidence, "faking it" to avoid exposure, and taking on an expert position even when I felt inept. I do not want people to know when I feel weak. Self-doubt leads me to silence and isolation. However, when I choose silence, I miss an opportunity to risk vulnerability and normalize the experience for myself and others. That semester, I experimented with sharing this experience, and the feedback from colleagues was the assurance that they feel this way, too. I was ready to ask for help.

Transitioning to Live Supervision

As therapy began to stall, I was mystified about why he was still going out with other women while we were working so hard to save the relationship. About this time, our clinic went through a transition. We moved locations and the hours of operation shifted all my clients to one day and two nights. I scrambled to reschedule the couple and he was angry. I was trying to move them from 6pm one weeknight to 7pm another weeknight, and he wasn't having it. I was having a strong reaction to his fury over the schedule change. I felt unappreciated, and was unaccustomed to being the target of a client's temper. I had logged more hours researching, preparing, and seeking supervision on this case than any other. My supervisor suggested I refer them out.

I felt a bitter mix of relief and failure as my own exit ramp approached. I spent an hour looking for another emotionally focused couple therapist who worked on a sliding scale in the same part of town, but I might as well have been looking for a mythical creature. I sent him three names, concerned that their prices and locations would be an obstacle.

She called me a day later, saying she suspected his refusal to move their time slot was a ploy to get out of couple therapy. She wasn't going to allow that, and they were coming at the new time after all. Mercifully, it was at a time when I could ask for live supervision. I jumped at the chance to bring in reinforcements when I felt in over my head.

With my supervisor acting as co-therapist, we mapped their cycle again and again, this time with a more experienced therapist at my side. That was affirming, as it wasn't terribly different than what I had been doing. My supervisor was more adept at stopping the reactive dance and blocking their avoidance of strong vulnerable emotions. They liked to retreat into the facts, staying with their negative perceptions. "He's still talking to other women," and "she's too cold," eventually gave way to more primary emotions and deep-rooted fears. However, even with the voice of experience in the room, the relationship dissolved. After months of therapy, and in the face of additional attachment wounds, the female partner decided the relationship was not salvageable. When her motivation to change the relationship wilted, the therapy abruptly ended.

Reflections on the Exit

There are times when I still feel conflicted about the case. In hindsight, there may have been a warning sign something was off balance. *Had I not accurately assessed both of their motivations for coming? Had I missed some coercion in the process?* In the end, I may not know; however, I learned something tremendously valuable. Therapists cannot want their clients to change more than the clients want it. It will not work. And oh, how I wanted them to change! How I wanted them to see the deeper attachment needs of the other; to soften, restore hope, and draw close to one another.

My disappointment in their ending therapy was tied to my signature theme. I wanted to prove I could help them. I wanted to prove my competence and usefulness, and gain their approval. I wanted to do meaningful work. I was so invested in saving the couple that I may have blinded myself to the more obvious work. Ultimately, the therapy helped them discover what they really wanted: to dissolve the relationship, because their motivation to repair it was already gone. They were ready to exit the relationship, and the therapy was part of their journey.

Had I not been already raising awareness of my underlying fear of incompetence, this would have been a more difficult and personal defeat. Being able to parse out the meaning of the conclusion of therapy and assign it to its rightful place made it much easier to pick myself up and move forward with my next case.

Couple #2: Introductions and Initiating Therapy

Daniel and Betty had been married for 57 years. She came into the clinic moving slowly with a walker, and always wore a pretty hat. Daniel, attentive and patient, obviously adored Betty, opening doors for her and helping her get settled for each session.

They adopted their only son, Ben, from a children's home at two days old, after 17 years of waiting. He was the light of their life. They rarely saw him now, though; he married Sami, a trial lawyer from New Jersey, 15 years ago. Ben traveled frequently as a successful consultant, and lived on the west coast, thousands of miles from his parents. Ben and Sami had chosen not to have children.

Daniel and Betty reported that the relationship with their son and his wife had been difficult. Where Betty was genteel and soft-spoken, they characterized Sami as loud and direct. Betty admitted to being easily offended and struggled to understand her daughter-in-law. Daniel had tried to remain close to Ben, but perhaps out of loyalty to Betty, Daniel withdrew from the relationship with his son when conflicts got heated.

Betty was also dying. She had collapsed at home last spring, and when doctors tried to rule out a stroke, they discovered her brain tumor. Glioblastoma IV is the most aggressive, advanced grade of the gliomas. After an unsuccessful surgery to partially resect the tumor, she declined to participate in a clinical trial or do any chemotherapy. In July, the doctors estimated she would live for six months, and she wanted to spend them at home, not going for treatment.

Ben had flown out three times after Betty's diagnosis, and they had been keeping in touch via video calls. On a recent call, Ben informed his parents that he and his wife would be leaving for a three-week vacation to Africa and would not be available by phone. Soon after that, Betty claimed that Sami had verbally attacked her, and they ended the call. They were now barely in communication. Daniel and Betty were mystified by the rift and irritated by the timing of Ben's long trip, not knowing from day to day how Betty's cognitive abilities might decline. They came in for help navigating the turmoil of this relationship with their son and daughter-in-law at such a sensitive time, and they didn't have much time left.

I used a genogram to map the family and gain some understanding about the qualities of the family's relationships. Both Daniel and Betty claimed to have warm, affectionate relationships with Ben when he lived at home. Sami's family looked like the complete opposite. Where Ben was connected, Sami was cut off from her entire family-of-origin. Where Ben was nurtured and grew up in the church, Sami was physically and verbally abused, neglected, and grew up an atheist. From there, she joined the Navy, became an officer, and went on to law school.

I wondered what it must have been like for Sami to marry into this family whose expectations were so vastly different from her own experience. She had not known the kind of closeness Ben had with his parents. I was curious about how foreign and strange that might have felt, when her experience of family was a high-conflict context where she was not always safe.

Betty described early days with her new daughter-in-law in the family as "rocky," but they made progress forging a relationship. They were patient and persistent about inviting their daughter-in-law into family rituals and gatherings. A decade later, the couple shared that Ben had revealed that he was a sex addict. Betty and Daniel were heartbroken for the pain Ben caused Sami. They explained they supported the couple as Ben sought counseling at a residential treatment center, and they believed he was now in recovery. They had expected that their support of Sami during that ordeal would have resulted in a closer relationship, but the difficulties persisted. I could imagine that coming from a family where Sami could trust no one, and after experiencing a betrayal from her partner, these persistent parents-in-law may have seemed unusual.

Seeing all the cutoffs on Sami's side of the map was a pivotal moment for Daniel and Betty. Sami no longer spoke to a single person in her family-of-origin. They could suddenly understand how isolated and alone in the world their daughter-in-law might feel. Sami's choice of career, her personality traits, her distant manner, and her constant readiness for battle all made perfect sense in the context of her family story of abuse, isolation, and abandonment. I shared a hypothesis aloud about whether their recent fight over that video call, when Sami verbally attacked Betty, might be part of a replicating pattern of distancing that Sami had used to protect herself from relational pain all her life. If Betty was the kindest, most constant version of a mother Sami had ever had, the prospect of Betty's death might have been uncomfortable enough to bring about another cutoff.

Another process I used in therapy was end-of-life relationship completion work. Using Ira Byock's model (1997) for palliative care and anticipatory grief, we worked through five things people often need to say for relationships to feel complete: I forgive you, please forgive me, thank you, I love you, and goodbye. It was through this conversation that, ultimately, Betty decided she needed to try to reconcile her relationship with Sami and Ben before the end of her life. Betty wrote a letter to Sami and sent it off, asking for forgiveness for the ways she had hurt her daughter-in-law. Sami wrote back, wishing her peace at the end of her life, but declined any further contact.

At that point in therapy, Ben came through town on a work trip. I invited him to join us for a family therapy session, and he agreed. I brought my supervisor in once again, knowing this might be my only chance. It felt like such an important session, and I was nervous about what was at stake. I wanted to see this family reconcile before my client's time was up.

I started the session by joining with Ben, sharing how his parents had conveyed their pride and love for him, and thanking him for being willing to take a risk in coming to see his parents' therapist, a stranger to him. I asked if he would share his story of what the past few months had been like for him.

Tears poured down his face as he described getting the devastating phone call, rushing to arrange a flight, coming to his parents in the hospital, and finally learning of her prognosis. He cared deeply for his parents and was struggling to accept the coming loss of his mother.

Concluding Therapy and Goodbyes

As we listened to Ben's account of where things went wrong between his wife and his mother, he had the appearance of a man trapped between a rock and a very hard place. Defending his bride and offending his dying mother, or taking his mother's side and distancing from his wife, whom he had worked so hard to win back after his infidelity. In that session, I saw a perspective of Betty that I had not seen before – a mother whose rejection of every reframe belied the enmeshment she still clung to with her son. She had not truly let him leave home yet. She was fighting for him to belong to her.

In that session, she was inflexible, unmoved by the supervisor beside me who was highlighting the perspective of her son and introducing the possibility that she had not truly known him as an adult, especially since he had been in recovery and was no longer struggling through his addiction. Ben told a different version of events, one about how his parents would brush minor offenses by Sami under the rug until they became intolerable, then erupt in anger, leaving Sami blindsided. Sami preferred to be direct in any moment of offense. Ben explained how Betty and Daniel's communication pattern seemed deceptive to her. It became clear that Betty was unwilling to consider this point, refusing to accept responsibility for her part in the rift, however small. She needed to be right about demonizing Sami, even if it meant sacrificing the little time she might have left with her son.

We did not accomplish the reconciliation that we had set out for in the session. Ben was unwilling to try to persuade Sami to talk with his mother, preferring to honor her decision to "leave them in peace." The following session would be our last as I found myself, yet again, watching a client take an early exit.

Betty and Daniel came in angry the following week. I braced myself. They blamed me for the failure of the joint session, rejecting my supervisor's interventions and claiming that I had let them down. They assumed I would be "running the show," and they were disappointed that I had given the reins over to a therapist who didn't know them. While I understood their complaint, I also knew that she was the right person to oversee that process. I trusted her voice of experience. Her perspective was less biased and her alliance more balanced.

I slowed them down, and their anger softened as I began telling them a story about the day I read their intake paperwork. I shared that I had seen Betty's illness was terminal, and I worried because my Achilles' heel is getting too close to my clients. I liked them immensely and I knew it would be a tough case. I knew it would be hard for me to care for someone, knowing they were dying. At the time, my supervisor had pulled me aside to say that she suspected they might be coming in to seek validation in initiating a cutoff so that they could live the remainder of Betty's days at peace instead of in turmoil.

Both were correct – I did care for them; it was painful. And, they were, ultimately, seeking to cut off their daughter-in-law, and would be fine living the rest of their lives without more drama and chaos. This was what the couple had genuinely wanted in the end. We just didn't get there the way I expected. First, Betty and Daniel had needed to try to make the repair.

This case touched on my signature theme of feeling incompetent in several ways. First, caring for clients decades older, with vast life experience, was intimidating. However, this time, I experienced gains in confidence as I saw light bulbs turn on, as they had with the couple's genogram and our anticipatory grief work. I believe this was meaningful therapy, and I am proud of the collaborative alliance we formed.

Hearing out an angry client and tolerating their dissatisfaction with an important session was a growing experience for me. It was a tough moment, but I found that I did not fall apart. Asking for a more experienced co-therapist to guide the session was the right thing to do at that stage in my development as a new therapist. I stood my ground in our final meeting. I acknowledged their disappointment and still managed to salvage the therapeutic alliance. At the conclusion of our final session, they asked for my personal contact information. They wanted to be able to get in touch when Betty died, so that I could be included in her memorial service. I told them to please call the clinic and that they would know how to reach me. I was touched. Even though they were telling me that I had not done the job that they had hired me to do, and even though they had come in "spitting mad," Daniel wanted to invite me into their grief. It was a powerful affirmation of the work we had accomplished together.

Reflections on the Exit

In the end, failing to repair the relationship with his mother allowed Ben to grow in his ability to tolerate his mother's disapproval. Initially, it felt like I had failed to bring about the positive change for which the family came in. However, again, I saw that I could not want the relationship to be repaired more than the client. The system did change, but not in the way I had planned.

I was sad that I could not help them repair the relationship with their son and daughter-in-law. I wanted to be good enough to guide them in restoring what was broken. However, in this case, there was never a strong bond with Sami, and I must believe that I did the best I could with what they brought in. If their daughter-in-law was unwilling to work on the relationship, and Betty was determined to keep her firmly in a one-down position, then there was no more I could do to help them bridge the gap. We moved into discussions on what forgiveness and acceptance might offer, and they were ready to exit.

6

GIVING BACK
A Therapist's Fears Not Revealed

Sharla Austin

Supervision Issues by Connie S. Cornwell

In supervising interns, one asks, "Did I miss something?" *Did I not see Sharla's anxiety?* I assumed Sharla was doing fine. I missed that this self-reliant intern, afraid to appear incompetent, really was needing to ask for help. I did not reinforce with Sharla that it is ok to struggle, and it is ok to ask for help. Isomorphism was alive and well as the clients were caught in a struggle, the therapist became caught, and, in my case, I was caught unaware there was a struggle.

It becomes a shared experience for everyone in the system: as the family is feeling incompetent in solving their own problems, the therapist can feel a lack of competence in her skills, and the competence of the supervisor is also tested. Regarding this case, I decided, in hindsight, that I should have been more inquisitive. I could have questioned Sharla more about how she really felt about this case. I trusted she could handle it. However, I had not considered at what cost to her. I could have asked more about how the case was progressing and, instead of assuming, I could have asked Sharla if she was comfortable with the content presented in therapy. During times of discomfort for the therapist, I must evaluate whether I have built the safety, security, and the connection with the supervisee for her to come to me with her concerns. Yet, in a paradoxical way, my not knowing Sharla's anxieties, and seeing her as a capable and competent therapist, may have been the balm she needed.

Giving Back

I am a wife, mother, and an eternal optimist, and I believe that we are all wired for, need, and desire to be in relationships with others. It is because of this belief, and the pain that I have personally witnessed resulting from broken relationships, that I decided to go back to school to become a couple and family therapist. At the time of this case I was two semesters away from graduating with a master's degree in family therapy. I was working at a clinic that specializes in training family therapists and provides therapeutic services on a sliding fee scale to increase access to care.

Pre-Therapy Panic

I am a creature of habit. Every day at the clinic, my routine was to walk into the office and immediately check my mailbox to see if I had any new intake forms. My general feelings upon receiving a new intake were those of anticipation, excitement, and curiosity; today was no different. I sat down at my desk with the intake form and started to read. At first, nothing unusual jumped out. It indicated that Andrew and Catherine, parents, and an 18-year-old son, Michael, were seeking therapy. They were referred by an internal psychiatry resident who had recently been working with Michael. My eyes traveled down the intake form to the section entitled "Presenting Problems," and I could not help but notice that every single line was full. Despite my little experience, I knew this was most likely a bad sign. I immediately felt a bit of anxiety beginning to well up as I started to read. My eyes soon fixated on the words "transgender ideation" and "hospitalized for suicidal tendencies," and I began to panic.

I immediately began formulating a way to diplomatically ask my supervisor to please reassign this case to someone else, when I heard a knock on the office door. Before I had a chance to say, "Come in," the door was opened, and my supervisor entered the office to specifically talk about the referral. I don't know if it was intentionally planned, but it was as if she timed her entrance. She gave me just enough space to read the intake form and let it sink in a little, but not enough time to devise how I was going to convince her to let me get out of it.

Normally, when my supervisor talked to me about a difficult case that I had been assigned, I would walk away feeling better and I was hopeful that this would be the same. I don't remember all the specifics of our conversation, but I do remember that she informed me that Catherine specifically requested a Christian therapist since she and her husband were devout Catholics. The mother had indicated that she and her husband did not believe that Michael was "truly transgender," but rather thought that their son was struggling with some unresolved issues from the past and this is how it was manifesting. My supervisor explained that she had informed Catherine that the clinic did not provide Christian counseling, but that we did have Christian therapists. Reportedly, this explanation was enough for Catherine. My supervisor informed me that, due to this specific request, she thought I would be a good therapist to work with this family.

I am not sure if my supervisor intended for this to be a vote of confidence with the aim of reducing the anxiety that she was sure I must be feeling but, if so, it did exactly the opposite. I am sure that we discussed a few more details about the case, but because of my fog of panic, it's all a bit hazy. I do remember that my supervisor left me with her famous line, which she uses with her supervisees when discussing particularly challenging clients: "What a great case!" I might have mustered a weak smile, but all I could think was, *The hell it is.*

Pre-Therapist Origins

I think it's important to expand on what exactly was giving me such massive amounts of anxiety. When I was reading the presenting problem section on the intake form my eyes were particularly drawn to the phrase "transgender ideation." Michael was born a boy but identified as a girl. Within the past six months, Michael's parents became aware of their child's transgender identification and they were vocal in expressing their skepticism and their religious objections.

I grew up in the Deep South, in the heart of the Bible Belt. While gender identity and sexual orientation were never explicitly discussed in my family-of-origin, we were deeply involved in the church. The prevailing message there was that anything that deviated from "normal" sexual orientation and gender identity was a sin. Of course, these topics were not discussed openly but rather in hushed voices, adding more stigma. I am more open-minded now, and these conservative church beliefs no longer resonate with me personally. But, if I am honest, I continue to be somewhat uncomfortable when directly facing these issues. I still carry a residue from my past which quietly whispers that these taboo topics are best avoided.

In addition, prior to going back to school to pursue a family therapy education, I was the youth director at a small church in south Alabama whose members were very conservative. I loved my job, and the members of the congregation (some I had known since childhood), but the longer I was there the more I realized that my views on certain topics, including sexual orientation, deviated from many of theirs. I am not proud of it, but, at the time, I avoided conversations regarding gender identity and sexual orientation. I feared that my job would be in jeopardy if the leadership of the church discovered my stance.

Part of the angst that I was feeling about this case was due to these past experiences. *How could I help this family have open and meaningful conversations about such a personal, painful, and sensitive topic when I was not fully comfortable with the subject matter myself?* In addition, I did not want the parents to have the expectation that I would join them in a mission to convince their child that she was not transgender. I also did not want their child to assume that because I was a Christian I would be sitting in a place of condemnation and judgment, or as her parents' co-conspirator.

The other troubling information on the intake form was where it indicated that Michael had previously, on several occasions, attempted suicide and had been hospitalized for "suicidal tendencies." Like so many, my life has personally been touched by the tragic impact of suicide. I know the heartbreak and pain of those who go on living after losing a loved one to suicide. Surprisingly, this is not the reason why

I was uncomfortable working with this family. Instead, it was my fear of being put on the spot.

To clarify – I cannot tell you the number of times, in different contexts, that I have heard a well-intentioned person make a comment along the lines of, "Everyone has at least thought about attempting suicide once in their life." Or, "I'm sure everyone in this room, at some point in time, has considered ending their life." Every time I hear a comment like that, I feel self-conscious, because I have never considered suicide. I can feel myself shrinking as I pray that their next comment will not be something like, "Raise your hand if you have ever thought about ending your life." I envision every hand in the room going up except mine and, for some weird reason, I imagine feeling horribly ashamed because of it. I do not mean to be insensitive, nor am I making light of a painful subject. I am simply being honest and truthful about how I have felt when those comments have been made. I have had periods of immense emotional pain and heartache but, even in those dark moments, I have never thought about ending my life. I understand what people are trying to do when they make those comments. They are trying to communicate to people who have had suicidal thoughts that these dark thoughts are not uncommon, to decrease feelings of isolation. I appreciate these motivations and I think that the good these comments hopefully accomplish outweighs the personal aloneness that I feel in those moments.

Sitting in my office, I thought that the child's suicidality would be a dominant topic in therapy. I worried that I would be pushed by the family to disclose whether it was something that I had ever struggled with personally. Mentally, my mind can comprehend things getting so bad in someone's life that it appears that suicide is their only option. I have even thought about scenarios in my own life where, if certain things happened, I do not know how I could go on living. Nonetheless, since I have not personally reached the point where I have contemplated suicide, I wondered whether this would serve as a barrier between me and this client. Suicide is such a deeply personal, far-reaching, and, depending on one's beliefs, eternal act. I worried that a lack of shared experience with someone who has genuinely contemplated or attempted suicide, or who is currently suicidal, might hinder my ability to be effectively therapeutic.

First Session Failings

I had a week to stew between receiving the intake form and meeting the family for the first time. Thankfully, I was busy with coursework from my classes and a new baby at home to keep me from becoming overwhelmed by the anticipation. The day before I was to meet with the family for our first session, I received a phone call from Catherine to let me know that she and Andrew would be in attendance the next day but, because of an illness, Michael would not be joining us. It would be disingenuous not to admit that I was incredibly thankful that Michael was under the weather. In my mind, I thought that meeting with the parents would allow me to get my toes wet with the family, rather than jumping all the way in right at the beginning.

Another security blanket that I was relying on was the fact that filling out paperwork can be quite time-consuming during the first session with clients. When the parents arrived, I warmly greeted them and ushered them back to one of our rooms. I doubt that I have been more thorough with any of my other clients when explaining the purpose of all the forms that they had to complete prior to us diving into their story. Once I handed the paperwork over, Catherine diligently began providing the necessary information. From the beginning, it was undeniable that Andrew was highly uncomfortable and anxious about being there, while Catherine exuded a soothing, warm, and gentle presence. I am exceptionally good at hiding my anxiety, so I doubt that they could sense what I was feeling internally; when nervous, I tend to overcompensate by exuding a very cool, calm, and collected demeanor. But, my anxiety was through the roof.

As Catherine was busy writing away, the two terrified people in the room were left to sit and wait. Typically, I use this time to review what paperwork has already been completed and collect my thoughts, but Andrew was unable to endure the silence. He began engaging in small talk with me to try to ease his discomfort. Reflecting on this conversation, I do believe that filling the silence helped him manage his anxiety, but I think he also saw it as an opportunity to try to gather some information about me.

I think it's important to mention that, with all my other clients, I have been very intentional about limiting the amount of self-disclosure

I engage in. In addition, clients are usually so wrapped up in their own drama that they are not interested in mining details about their therapist's life. Now, I do not remember everything that we discussed in that first conversation, but there are a few things that stick out. Andrew was curious about my education; understandable, because all clinicians in my office were either students or recent graduates. When he began this line of questioning, rather than just keeping the conversation isolated to my master's degree, I seized the opportunity to volunteer information about where I pursued my undergraduate degree. While I am not Catholic, I did go to a well-respected Catholic university, which I thought would be interesting, appealing, and hopefully impressive to them.

In what I can only say was an attempt to impress the couple further, I shared with them (unprompted) that my sister was a Georgetown graduate and my cousin was a Notre Dame graduate. The fact that both I and two close members of my family held degrees from Catholic universities was certainly pertinent information, and enhanced my credibility as a therapist ... right? As the conversation became chattier, I additionally disclosed that I grew up in southern Alabama and that my undergraduate degree was in marketing. I also thought it would be good to highlight the fact that I was in youth ministry for many years, prior to going back to school for my master's. I can only determine that my motivation to self-disclose was to let the couple know, not-so-subtly, that I was the Christian therapist they had been looking for.

As Andrew and I bounced from one subject to the next, Catherine would chime in from time to time, joining us in a conversation that resulted in taking longer to complete the paperwork. Obviously, I was not too bothered by that fact and neither did they seem to be. There were times where I could feel my internal voice telling me to stop talking, especially about myself. But, in that moment, my mouth was a runaway train that I could not stop.

After the first session was over, I worked to figure out why I volunteered as much information as I did. I realized that the longer I was able to drag out the conversation, the longer I could postpone diving into the issues that brought the family to therapy. I was not at peace about being their therapist, and the longer we engaged in idle conversation, the longer I was able to delay the inevitable. Sitting in the room with Andrew and Catherine during the first session, I was still so uncomfortable being their therapist that I engaged in a level of self-disclosure that I would advise anyone against today.

I do not believe that I divulged any information that should have disqualified me from continuing to work with the family. And, if you had asked the couple, I am sure they would tell you that this conversation helped reduce their level of anxiety. However, that could have been achieved in a manner that did not put "me" as the central focus. While it was not my plan to intentionally craft a scenario that resulted in delaying the start of "real" therapeutic conversations, much less engage in a conversation that revolved around me, I did selfishly seize the opportunity when Andrew opened the door. I accepted the "invitation," when I should have gently and therapeutically built rapport with them in a way that did not prioritize my need to assuage my own anxieties. Now that I am removed from this case and have a bit more therapeutic wisdom, it is abundantly clear that if I had utilized supervision to process my anxieties, fears, and concerns prior to my first session, I would have been better able to soothe my nerves and interact with the couple in a more professional and appropriate manner.

After all my failings in the first session, I wish I could say that I walked away feeling more at ease with these clients; unfortunately, that did not happen. During our initial encounter, Andrew mentioned that one of his brothers was a therapist. I will admit that there were a few choice exclamatory words that immediately came to mind as my thoughts began to spiral out of control. He informed me that he had discussed the difficulties they were experiencing as a family with his brother, who then encouraged them to seek therapy. Rather than finding comfort in knowing that they had a supportive family member to encourage them through the process, my mind immediately jumped to the worst-case scenario. I was instantly terrified that Andrew would pick up the phone and debrief with his brother after each of our therapy sessions and I would, inevitably, be critiqued. I was convinced that my inexperience would be exposed through these conversations, and I was sure that Andrew's brother would render the verdict that I was an incompetent therapist. I felt completely vulnerable and I just knew that I was going to end up humiliated.

Moving Forward

In discussing this case with my supervisor, she highlighted the importance of allowing Michael to address the "transgender" label that his parents were concerned about. Rather than making assumptions, my supervisor stressed that Michael should have the opportunity to accept or deny that label, and expand on how the label might, or might not, be a fit for her. In addition, my supervisor reminded me to always *stay curious*. Did she want to be referred to as "he" or "she"? Did she want to be referred to by her given name or did she have another name that she would prefer to use? If Michael did identify as transgender, how did she come to this conclusion? Did she want to transition? The list of questions that my supervisor spouted off left her mouth much faster than I could write them down, but they were extremely helpful. During this supervision session, I realized that my own fears and concerns about this case were causing me to have tunnel vision on "issues," rather than remembering that these were hurting human beings. My preoccupation with my own fears and anxieties was preventing me from being truly present with this family. I knew I needed to step back and approach this family with an open mind and a renewed sense of curiosity.

After this supervision session, I felt like I would be able to set aside my "self-of-the-therapist" issues and attend to the needs of the family in a professional and therapeutic manner. After the first session, I was more concerned that Michael would see me as a parental ally, rather than as a neutral therapist and possible advocate. To try to ease any of these potential concerns, I was intentional in being transparent with her about what her parents had shared with me the week before about her, and their motivations for seeking therapy. I trod carefully. I wanted to convey respect for Michael and to let her know that her voice and input would be valued and heard in therapy.

During our next session, with Andrew, Catherine, and Michael present, Michael expressed ambivalence toward being in therapy with her parents. She was frank in verbalizing her skepticism about their motivations, and shared her doubt that therapy would accomplish anything of value. She indicated that there were rifts in her relationships with her parents, but expressed they were something that she had accepted and did not have aspiration for, nor hope of, improving. She presented as very disengaged from her parents, the therapeutic process, and any hope of positive growth.

This was not the first time that I had had a client express skepticism or a lack of desire for things to improve, so I was not deterred. I love a challenge, and I was determined that Michael's nonchalant attitude was not going to discourage me. I soldiered on, and remained intentional in attending to the therapeutic relationship with her. At the end of this second session, I acknowledged that she had every right to be reticent, but I asked her to give it a try anyway. She agreed to participate in the process with an open mind. Now, with all parties expressing a willingness to proceed, we were able to begin the hard work of therapy.

From the beginning, I really struggled with correctly gendering Michael with my use of pronouns, especially in the first several sessions. It was difficult to have an individual who looked and spoke like a "he," but wanted to be referred to as "she." When I first started working with Michael, I mistakenly referred to her as "he" and "him" numerous times and each time I would get flustered and frantically apologize, which only made things more awkward. She would quickly accept my apology and we would all barrel ahead in therapy.

After several sessions, I decided that I needed to change my reaction if I were to misgender her again. I was struggling because this was new and foreign to me and I wanted to be honest with her. Of course, it did not take long for me to slip up. Rather than giving her a knee-jerk apology, I paused and looked at her and said,

> I need you to know that when I refer to you as "he" and "him" it is because this is new for me and I struggle at times. I really do apologize, and my intention is not to be disrespectful toward you. I hope that you will be gracious with me in my fumbling.

For the first time in therapy with Michael, I saw a slight smile cross her lips as she nodded in understanding.

I refined my hypotheses about the issues that were driving the painful interactions in this family over the next several sessions. I hypothesized that Michael had not felt genuinely loved, valued, nor accepted by her father for much of her life. In addition, I wondered whether she felt betrayed by her mother because Catherine did not consistently stand up to Andrew on behalf of Michael. I wanted to decrease the emphasis on Michael's gender identification and depression, and refocus the family on the broken relationships and hurt between them. I also wanted to reestablish broken lines of communication within the family. It was apparent to me that tough and difficult issues were avoided, and assumptions were driving forces in their interactions (or lack of inter-actions) with one another.

Therapeutic Outcomes

I am proud of the work that was accomplished with this family, even though I felt like more work could have been done. I believe that therapy humanized Michael in the eyes of Andrew and Catherine, and in my eyes. The parents entered therapy full of fear and love for Michael. They also carried an enormous amount of frustration, sadness, grief, and guilt. These intense emotions, related to their child's trans-gender identification and her ongoing battle with depression, were all-consuming. They had monopolized Andrew and Catherine's interactions with Michael for years and had come to define their child. In the beginning, I, too, defined Michael by the presenting problems that scared and intimidated me. Through dialogue, vulnerability, and open-ness, therapy allowed us to connect with her in a way that fostered understanding and relational connectivity. Michael's depressive symp-toms lessened. She gradually began to engage with the family and started cooking and riding her bike – activities that she had stopped participat-ing in for a long time. She was engaging with her parents in non-combative exchanges.

In addition, Andrew and Catherine were able to express anxieties and fears that they had about Michael's transgender identification, devoid of moralistic arguments. They clearly and lovingly expressed their worry and, as a result, Michael was able to listen and connect with her parents rather than respond from a place of feeling attacked and judged. Ultimately, the parents decided that their need to be right was not more important than their child's need to feel fully loved and valued. They communicated this message to Michael verbally and, to demonstrate their support in a tangible way, they decided to contribute financially toward her laser hair removal.

Andrew eventually expressed regretting some of his parenting choices, and Michael's resulting behavior through the years. Andrew acknowledged the pain that he knew was a result of his actions and ultimately asked for forgiveness. While Michael accepted her father's apology, they both expressed uncertainty about how to move forward with their relationship. I highlighted the enormity of the relational transaction that had just occurred and assured them that it was perfectly understandable that they continued to feel somewhat uncomfortable with one another. I wanted to jump up and down and celebrate what had just happened, but I could sense that my exuberance did not match their emotions and tempered my response.

Further Reflections

This case was not the first time that my supervisor had demonstrated much greater confidence in my abilities than I had had in myself. This was, however, the first time that I had desperately wanted to find a way to get out of working with a family. In hindsight, I should have been forthcoming with my supervisor about the level of anxiety I truly had about this family, right from the start. While I am an introspective person who can self-evaluate, it still would have been beneficial to talk about my concerns with my supervisor before I ever met with the family for our first session. I pride myself on being competent and self-sufficient in many areas of my life. I value these qualities in myself and they have served me well but, as I have gotten older, I can also see how they have prevented me from admitting areas of weakness that I did not want exposed. In retrospect, I withheld my fear and how ill-equipped and anxious I felt, because I did not want to appear incompetent nor admit how much help I really needed with this case.

In addition, I wish that I had been more transparent with my supervisor. While I believe therapy was beneficial for this family, and that they were pleased with what was accomplished, I wonder what else might have been gained if I had worked through my self-of-the-therapist reactions. I was asking my clients to be vulnerable and express their fear and pain, but I was not willing to do the same with my supervisor. It is critical for therapists-in-training to fully engage in the process of super-vision to work through things that might prevent us from being fully present and available to our clients. This growth-oriented approach helps us with our current clients, as well as our future clients.

Another important lesson that I learned from this experience was that even when I feel completely incompetent as a therapist, I can still be effective. With this family, I felt like I was treading water much of the time and, still, positive strides were made. As was my routine, in our termination session, I spent a lot of time highlighting the family's strengths and what they had accomplished. The family acknowledged that they had reached their therapeutic goals and reported that they were leaving therapy optimistic and hopeful.

As our final session ended, Andrew and Catherine reflected on their experience of me as their therapist. They expressed gratitude that I was the therapist that was assigned to work with them during such a difficult season in their lives. I was so moved as they affirmed and encouraged me as a therapist-in-training and offered blessings as I continued the journey. I was humbled and felt unworthy, but was so appreciative of their kind words. I did not solicit their feedback, but believe it was a providential blessing meant for me to hear. I had initially dreaded working with this family and would have given a limb for my supervisor to reassign them to a different therapist. But, in the end, being their therapist was truly a gift; this trio gave me back at least as much as I gave them. I have never felt as inadequate as a therapist as I did when I started working with Andrew, Catherine, and Michael, and I have never felt so affirmed in the calling to become a therapist as I did when we ended our time together.

7

CLOSE TO HOME
Learning to Detach When the Clients Are a Mirror

Shirley Shropshire

Supervision Issues by Connie S. Cornwell

Learning family therapy can be a struggle. As a supervisor, I question whether I need to directly intervene in a case and rescue the therapy intern, or hold back. I weigh whether intervening will have a negative impact on developing the intern's self-confidence against whether it is needed for the benefit of the clients. I feel I must support the growth of the therapist and take care of the clients at the same time. The struggle is worthwhile when it opens the door to processing self-of-the-therapist issues for both the therapist and supervisor.

As the supervisor, I must be aware of whether I am becoming too involved. Am I overprotecting the therapist? Or am I concerned about the reputation of the clinic and wish to keep the referral sources satisfied? The clinic where I supervise is part of a large medical school that feeds us clients. These shared clients report satisfaction, or dissatisfaction, to the physicians that refer to the clinic. Thus, it is always in the back of my mind, as I want to train competent therapists, provide good service to our clients, and satisfy our referral sources. In Shirley's case, the referral came from a community crisis team that was beginning to utilize our services, so I had the need to demonstrate the effectiveness of family therapy.

For the intern, struggles with a difficult and intimidating family member can trigger problems and patterns of dysfunction within the therapist's family-of-origin. It is also easy for the beginning therapist, eager to be helpful, to get lost in the system. The new therapist can get sucked into the clients' pattern(s)/dances and become stuck.

These triggers are not good or bad, if the therapist is aware. It is when one is unconscious and blind to them, that problems are created for the therapist. The therapist can become ineffective, such as when she fails to remain neutral and sympathizes with one family member more than the others, does not deal with a certain topic the family is clearly avoiding, fails to see the family as a system, or joins the family in seeing one member as the problem. It is easy to catch the family's disease when the therapist unwittingly over-identifies with the family, as in this case where the clients reflected Shirley's own family.

Supervision focused on how to extricate Shirley from the case by helping her to take distance and look through a larger systems lens. The therapist was aided in examining what about the case felt familiar and whether there was a specific family member that was difficult. For this case, I supported a conversation with Shirley to explore self-of-the-therapist issues. What did she experience in the room with the family that was a block or barrier for her?

Shirley identified how the family she was treating was like her own family – same family life stage, and children with chronic health issues and behavior challenges. She was able to see the overlaps and process her concerns about her family, separate from the case family. She learned how to use her own experience as a mom with children dealing with chronic illness to connect with the family and guide them in needed changes. The key intervention was to teach her about what I call "divine detachment," which is the ability to care while remaining detached and not focused on the therapy outcome. Shirley was able to empower the parents to confront their challenges, rather than carry their burden for them. Through my modeling detachment, space was created for Shirley to grow without worrying about the results, which in turn gave space for the clients to discover their best selves. As therapists, we do not know better than the clients what they need, what they are here to learn, or what they should do. We create space for clients to discover what is best for them and avoid becoming personally attached, so that the therapy does not become the therapist's agenda, but rather the client's healing.

Close to Home

"It's your fault that I'm like this." These were the scorching words of my teenage son to my husband. In the moment that my husband told me of the conversation with our son, I remember a sinking feeling in the pit of my stomach. Even though I wasn't present, I too was burned when the words fell from my husband's lips. I froze. When I was able to reflect, I remember being so grateful that I wasn't present when my son said it. Perhaps having to hear it firsthand would have been even worse. It was painful and even frustrating. Even though I knew my son struggled with issues of appearance, I did not want to hear how he blamed me and my husband. What was I supposed to do? This was the part of our journey I most feared facing.

I had returned to graduate school later in life to become a marriage and family therapist. I had started my career in public education and then stayed home to care for my three young children. By the time I returned to school, my children were older. I was a serious student, fully embracing the rigor of graduate education. When I was enrolled in a family-of-origin course, I poured myself into process papers and my own family genogram. Throughout my education, professors consistently addressed self-of-the-therapist issues. I challenged myself to work on my personal relationships, learn my family history, and create more beneficial relationships. In the process, I convinced myself that I was inoculated from any interference which might arise in a therapy session. I had processed my life until I felt like there was nothing left to process. I filed my personal essays away and began internship with excitement.

As a student, I started clinical work with cases swimming around in my head and evoking such anxiety that I would struggle to fall asleep at night. I progressed to restful nights accompanied by increased confidence in myself and by my third semester of internship, I had become a more assured therapist. I was learning Emotionally Focused Couple Therapy (Johnson, 2005), in part through a course specifically focused on integrating EFT skills into therapy. I had learned enough about myself as a therapist to know the model was a fit for me. So much so, that I was beginning to use it in my work with families, most of whom were referred by area schools.

Introductions and Overlaps

When I first met the Parkers, I immediately felt connected. The parents were both educators: Ellen was a 31-year-old college professor and Bob was a 32-year-old middle school teacher. The family included three children, John, age 10, Mark, age 7, and Rachel, age 4. All biblical names, just as my own. Rachel mimicked my own youngest daughter when she was the same age. The Parkers drove about 30 miles, from a rural suburb, just to find a therapist that would see them as a family. I, too, drove from a rural suburb. It was not lost on me that this family closely represented my own, when my children were younger.

The family entered therapy after Mark had taken a kitchen knife and wielded it in the air in an angry and desperate moment, prompting his parents to report the emergency. A crisis intervention team recommended that the Parkers seek family therapy. Of all the information I gathered from the family during our intake, it was the mother's description of Mark's disorder that triggered my internal alarm. Ellen explained that her son had become ill as an infant, with vomiting and diarrhea that lasted for more than a year, before doctors could determine the cause. She explained he had food issues and dietary restrictions specific to sugar. The parents described a horrific and traumatizing beginning to bringing their child into the world; however, they spoke of it with resignation and stoicism. For me, it was the period of one year without a diagnosis that didn't add up, in part because this all felt too familiar.

My eldest daughter and my son, second in order, were both born with a rare disease called Klippel-Feil Syndrome (KFS). It was my son's intense snoring that prompted me to take him to an otolaryngologist at the age of 1 to see if there was a problem. The otolaryngologist ordered an X-ray, which showed multiple fusions and anomalous features in his cervical and thoracic spine (neck and upper back). It marked the beginning of our journey. I was referred to my pediatrician and then to multiple specialists. It took six months to get an appointment with a genetic counselor at a nearby children's hospital, which was an improvement over the one-year wait at the first children's hospital we were referred to.

The genetic counselor informed me of my children's diagnosis. I was told that, though most KFS cases are sporadic, having two children with the condition was unusual and most likely genetic. This also meant that all our children carry a 50% chance of passing on the disorder. I still do not fully agree with the assessment of genetic risk, but I cannot escape knowing I am responsible for it. *Eight years* passed before our family encountered a pediatric orthopedist that had any experience with KFS. By that time, my family was used to doctors not knowing anything about KFS.

I had been a rare disease parent long enough to know that there were many things doctors could not tell me about my children. They could not tell me how my children would be impacted over their life. They could not tell me they could fix their spinal curves or fusions in their necks. They could not tell me what it meant for my children to have KFS. All they could tell me was that my children should not play contact sports or any physically aggressive sport that could risk injuring their necks, since neck injury could lead to paralysis more easily for my children. They told me that because my children did not start off with "normal" spines, there was not much that could be done to make them normal. As a mother, how could I look at my beautiful children and believe what I was told? For me, believing took time and knowledge.

In the early years of my children's diagnosis, at a time before the internet was user-friendly, I had scoured the web for information. When I found information, it was written for medical professionals. I was not deterred. I would decipher the jargon by looking up medical terminology, then read and reread to understand the information. Even now, there are no colorful brochures written in everyday language to explain KFS.

At the time of my children's diagnosis, I was in denial. But looking back, I get angry thinking about the genetic counselor showing me information in a medical textbook when my children were diagnosed. I get angry because I realize their disease is marginalized, forgotten, and unimportant. I discovered for myself that I was living in a vast context of insufficiency. No one, not one medical professional in all the years our family has dealt with KFS, has ever asked us how we are coping with two children having a rare disorder.

In my initial work with the Parker family, I sought supervision about conceptualizing the case. I was concerned about Mark's behavior and wanted to make sure I was intervening appropriately. However, Ellen and Bob were also concerned about their oldest child, John, who had autism and would become so dysregulated that the whole family would find themselves going in circles. Ellen attempted to solve both sons' problems by giving solutions which only escalated each person's anger, until finally Ellen would withdraw by walking away or going to her room. Bob would arrive home and attempt to help Ellen by taking her place in the cycle, before ultimately withdrawing when his own suggestions did not work. As I worked with this family, it was clear that the eldest son's autism and the middle son's rare metabolic disorder frequently attended the family's negative interaction cycle, or "merry-go -round" as we called it. The family felt like they were going round and round, in the same process, every time there was a problem; the parents' solutions only served to intensify each child's anger.

I distinctly remember John telling me during the first session that his family needed therapy because of him. His hands were cupped, his back slouched, and his face looking down as he cautiously peeked up at me, and then down again, to explain that it was his fault the family had to go to therapy. I responded to him by explaining that his family could not have believed it was all his fault, because everyone came to therapy together. I remember feeling as though I had to say something to lessen the burden he was carrying, but I'm not certain the reframe worked. I also wanted to show, early on, that my focus was the family, because the whole system needed to understand how each member was helping to maintain the cycle, and how to change it.

I remember having a lingering question in my head: *How on earth do these two sons see themselves so negatively?* John and Mark were cloaked in "bad" from head to toe, as though nothing could take the bad out of them. How did having a diagnosis lead to "bad"? I could see in the family's story that the sons often disliked how the parents responded to them, but the feeling in the room seemed so overwhelming, even stale. It was like the family hated this awful place they were in, but they were resigned to its control over them. What was the cycle that was keeping guilt so alive in this family that the two children with a diagnosis were "bad," and the parents felt so helpless and hopeless to solve it?

Personal and Professional

As a therapist, I knew that cases getting stuck in my head were an occupational hazard that came with the territory. Yet, with the Parkers, I found myself questioning both the process in the family, as well as the process of their involvement with other professionals treating their children. Did they feel confident enough to assert themselves as parents, ask questions, plan, follow medical advice?

In the beginning of my time with the Parkers, I did not focus much on my own experience as a rare disease parent. I was many years removed from my early difficulties and was comfortable exercising my voice, which the Parkers did not seem to be doing. I needed to know more about Mark's diagnosis, so I started by researching his metabolic disorder, hoping it would help me to understand more about what the family was dealing with daily. I had a hunch that what the parents described to me was not a common illness or food allergy. And, in my search, I found exactly what I had suspected: Mark's condition was rare.

In that moment, the confidence I had built over the previous two semesters was replaced with fear. I was caught in a paradox as a therapist. I was diligent to ask questions about health and include this information in genograms, and was even hyper-aware of clients' illnesses, recognizing some of them as rare diseases. However, the Parkers were different. Mark was the first child I'd had with a rare disease, and one that was seriously impacting him and his family. I understood what it was like to have a child with a rare disease and I felt paralyzed.

As a rare disease parent, I was well versed in the isolation and ambiguity of living with one. I had learned to just tell people that my kids have back and neck problems, because saying "Klippel-Feil Syndrome" would result in questioning looks that ultimately lead to saying "back and neck problems" anyway. When even medical professionals don't know about KFS, how could I expect a lay person to know? It was this subtle nuance of explanation that caught my attention with the Parker family. I was not led to consult an online resource because the family explicitly discussed Mark having a rare disease. Instead, I noticed the way the family explained the disease. They reported it took over a year to diagnose, the doctors could not figure it out, and when the family told me the name of the disease, and I asked questions, they explained it to me in lay terms. The Parkers never actually mentioned the word "rare" when describing the illness. Why would they? Rare diseases are figuratively and literally orphaned; not special, but plagued with difficulty.

When the fear firmly settled into my realization of all this family was facing, it left me scared to work with them. What did they not know about living with and managing a child with a rare disease? What was it like for them to parent a child with a rare disease and another with autism? What were they having difficulty facing? It took me years to learn, embrace, and understand the reality of a rare diagnosis; how could I help this family? It is one thing to look at a family and consider disease treatment and management when disease variables are known. It is altogether different when the journey is full of uncertainty, fraught with barriers, and devoid of treatment options.

I was an older student with plenty of life experience and I had diligently processed my own issues. It was not often in supervision that my own personal issues surfaced. I was doing my best to keep them at bay, because that's what I thought a professional therapist was supposed to do. Yet, I had to share with my supervisor that I was scared. I confessed to her that I had done all my family-of-origin work, and that I thought I was therefore protected against my own experiences coming up in therapy. My supervisor was a well-seasoned master; I wanted her to make all the fear go away. She explained to me that she understood what was happening. She could see how the "inoculation" had not worked; now the disease was leaking through and I could not contain it. She said, "Just because you're scared doesn't mean you can't do it."

In a nutshell, I loved and dreaded her guidance. I was accustomed to "scared" letting me off the hook because I could freeze or avoid, but my supervisor was wise to fearful, freezing people. She had taught me to maintain "workability." If I couldn't face feeling scared, how could the family? She insisted that even though I had fears, I could also validate this family from a place of lived experience in rare disease and parenting children with special needs. My supervisor told me to ask myself as a parent of a rare disease child, "What would I want someone to tell me?"

The weight of all my knowledge of rare disease challenges bore down on me. As a parent, I was still hurt when facing my own son's pain. What was I going to do when Mark's fear and pain showed up in the therapy room? I was scared about what might come up and how I would respond.

Mapping the Cycle

As I worked with the Parkers, I initially intervened with the parents and John. I began to expand the parents' experience of John. We began to map his primary emotions and perceptions when the family was caught in their cycle. John was a high-functioning student in an autistic class-room at school. One of the children in the class had extremely disruptive behaviors that bothered John and he described the student as "bad." John was able to discuss how he gets "melty" when he and his mother get caught on the "merry-go-round." He discussed how everything just "snaps" and then he "breaks" when his mom pulls away from him, which leads to him following her around. These experiences left John thinking he must be "bad," just like the kid in his class who nobody wants to be around.

A major shift in the family happened when John longingly looked at his parents and discussed how he wanted them to stay with him when he was "all melty." As a therapist, I will never forget the look on the parents' faces. They did not believe that they could possibly be what John needed. Bob and Ellen were so used to living with the inability to fix things that they believed the power to fix the family laid elsewhere. I knew how important it was for the parents to be able to stay with John and comfort him, yet I had to slow down and remind myself how powerless it can feel to not be able to "fix" what is wrong with your child and the challenges they face.

Remembering my own powerlessness, and getting back in touch with the pain it caused, helped me to validate and understand Bob and Ellen. Remembering my powerlessness also reminded me that I had grieved when my own children were diagnosed. I had grieved the loss of dreams I had for them and the difficulties they would face. In some ways, I realized I still occasionally grieved the inability to protect my children from a world that only saw people in terms of "normal" or "not normal." It made sense to me that the Parker parents always got caught up in trying to find solutions for their sons. For this family, the answers always laid outside of the parents. Even Ellen's beloved parenting books served as an outside expert. As parents, they were trying to fix things, because that is what parents are "supposed" to do.

In an early session, when therapeutic work was focused on the parents and John, I recall Ellen commenting, "When you have a child with special needs …" I interrupted her and said, "You have two children with special needs." She looked perplexed. I commented that I was a rare disease parent myself, and that Mark also had special needs. As a student therapist, I was slow to self-disclose any information and, in that moment, I almost did not think before the information came out of my mouth. My supervisor encouraged me to trust myself more in moments when I self-disclose. I know that telling the family that they have two children with special needs could seem like a terrible reframe, but it was not. Ellen said that she was "impressed." I realized that I was validating the difficulty that the parents were facing in their experience of living with a child diagnosed with a rare disease. The family felt so isolated in their illness experience. They lived in an everyday world that was unaware of their struggle. In fact, it was easier for the family to focus on John's autism because more of the public is familiar with this issue. I understood the difficulties that the family faced which enabled me to validate their reality. I had a unique situation that benefited my ability to connect with the Parkers, and I was able to use it in a way that contributed positively to therapy.

Moving toward Mark

Mid-phase in our work, the family was beginning to focus on interactions between Bob, Ellen, and Mark. For me, this meant I would have to face the possibility of Mark's pain. The moment that I feared the most had arrived; I knew that it was coming and it percolated in my mind for days. I knew that I would need to soothe myself, stay focused, and challenge myself to allow the moment to happen, to face the reality. In a way, I feared that Mark would blame Bob and Ellen the same way my own son had; that something painful would be said, and I would not know how to handle it as a therapist.

In supervision, I confessed to my supervisor what my own son had said. She probed me with a few questions, her elbow rested on her desk, and her hand positioned intellectually under her chin. She responded to me so assuredly and matter-of-factly: "Don't you see?" She went on to explain how of course my son could say what he was feeling to my husband, and that we must have been good parents for our son to know he could trust us with his feelings. I was dumbfounded. In all the pain, I could not see that my own child was able to reach out and let us know that he was hurting. When I pondered it further, I realized that my husband had faced my son's angry words and then responded to his pain and my son's deeper emotion. My husband stood in front of our hurting, accusatory child and, instead of reacting to my son's blame, he explained that if there was anything he could have ever done as a father to take away KFS, he would have done it. He explained that he could not, and he knew it hurt when other kids made hurtful comments. My husband had done the same thing that I was working so hard to accomplish with the Parkers, to help them be emotionally present with their children.

How had my supervisor looked inside my pain to know that I needed to be told that I was a good parent? I did need to know. I needed to see the strength in what had happened. I needed to see the strength in all the work that the Parkers had already done with John. They, too, needed to know that they were good parents. The more I pondered how muddy it can get, facing a hurt child's anger, the more I realized the reward of knowing it doesn't have to run the show. I realized how powerful it was for my husband to just be with our son in his pain in a way that says "Yes, I see. I see you hurting and it makes sense to me that you are hurting. I'm glad you could tell me about it and we could talk to one another." It helped me to stay focused and to realize that I was working to help Mark to not be alone in his fear, to help him begin to speak about it. I was also working to get Bob and Ellen to turn toward one another and care for each other while facing an angry, hurting child.

In one session, Mark was able to discuss his fear for the first time. In the Parker family, there were no discussions about Mark's illness. The topic was taboo, since it might possibly invoke Mark's anger and entice the family back to the "merry-go-round." Mark was accustomed to being alone in his experience and often used his anger to enact boundaries around food and to keep his parents away. I wasn't sure that I could get Mark to reveal anything, but I was determined to break the family rules and open any kind of conversation I could with Mark.

I began to ask Mark questions about what it was like when his illness made him feel sick. Mark was guarded but allowed me to ask him questions. He would give me tidbits of information as he squirmed and continually glanced at his parents. I tried to expand every tidbit he gave and spontaneously decided to ask him to elaborate by telling me the color of whatever he was describing. He talked about how he just wanted to be "normal" and normal was "pink." He talked about how in moments when he was ill he was "scared" and "terrified," even though he claimed that he did not know what "terrified" meant. I affirmed to him that he knew exactly what it meant. He talked about how "terrified" was "pitch-black." His parents had never heard him talk about his illness in that way. He acknowledged that he would often hide from his parents when he felt physically ill, since he might miss out on seeing his friends and being "normal." Although I was focused on Mark, I could see Bob and Ellen hanging on his every word, shushing the other kids to remain silent.

As our work progressed, it was clear that the parents would have to face Mark's anger and at the same time learn to speak to his fear. It was not going to be easy. Mark had been pushing back for years and Bob and Ellen had pulled back in response. Throughout therapy, the parents began to enact structure, including time-outs and family chores. The parents discussed how they had learned to be with John in his "experiencing." I remember the father describing how affirming it was that when he just listened to John tell about his bad day at school, this was enough for John to calm down and go about his day. The parents' success with John provided a road map for the work that they would have to do with Mark. They also began creating more boundaries around time for themselves as a couple, and I continued to encourage them to consider ways they might support and comfort one another as they faced Mark's anger.

In one of our later sessions, John discussed how he had had a good day. He had won first place in a race at school. He came to therapy grinning ear to ear. I encouraged him to tell his parents about his "good feelings." When I asked Bob and Ellen about discussing "good feelings" with the kids, they appeared confused. I asked them if John being labeled "autistic" had kept them from discussing "good feelings." The parents couldn't name what got in the way, but they commented that they had just never thought of it. I surprised myself when I asked them about the autism label. Later, when I reflected, I recalled how painful it was for me to see the words "Klippel-Feil Deformity" written on medical papers from a doctor's visit for my son. I was enraged and hurt at the same time. Deformity? Deformity! The label was painful. But, as a parent, I can choose how I see my child, and how I interact with my child in such a way that he can see beyond the label. As a parent, I get to choose to have a relationship with my child, not a label. I hoped that the Parker parents were able to do the same.

In the end, I had to refer the Parkers to another therapist. I was at the end of my internship and Bob and Ellen wanted to continue therapy as they worked on their relationship with Mark. It was not easy to refer this family to another therapist. It was painful to let go of the joy of witnessing this family's progress. I had the privilege of saying they were all important and needed, no matter how hard, and ugly, and muddy it got. I got to say, "I see you, I hear you, and I get you." I got to see Bob and Ellen realize they were important as parents, and got to see the rewards of powerful validation.

Reflections

Though I started out scared, I learned how fortunate I was to work with this family. I learned so much about myself. Of all the cases I had as a student, this case forced my personal growth as a therapist who is also a parent. I learned that my personal processing, no matter how hard I tried, could not be completed in neat and tidy essays that I finished in class and then filed away. As a therapist, personal processing never ends.

It intertwines with the work of families that will undoubtedly share experiences similar to my own.

This case forced me to face my struggles as a parent, to evaluate and reflect on what it really means to parent, what it means to parent a child with a physical issue, and to parent in the reality of a rare diagnosis that is chronic and incurable. I had learned how not to freeze, but instead to face my personal emotions in a way that was productive and contributed to my work as a therapist. Prior to working with the Parker family, I had undervalued my experience as a parent and my own experience as a parent of two children with a rare diagnosis. I realized that I had done to myself what society at large had done to rare disease: ignored it. I can laugh at myself now when I think of how futile it was to believe I could contain my personal issues and their intersections with my work as a therapist.

I also grew professionally with this case. As a beginning therapist, supervision is a lifeline for surviving the initial days and weeks of doing therapy. I realized with this case, and even more toward the end of my time as a student therapist, that supervision was no longer a lifeline. In fact, quite the opposite began to take place for me. I began to realize that there would be minor things that would not resonate with me from supervision. It could have been a suggested reframe or a part of a case conceptualization; mostly minor things that I would spend time processing and considering but inevitably conclude did not fit the case. I struggled with this at first because I was so accustomed to applying every tidbit of assistance from supervision directly to my cases.

As I began to reflect, I realized, theoretically, that it was my attunement to the Parker family, and other cases, that was influencing me to be more critical and judicious with supervision. In short, I learned to trust my own instincts and intuition about the clients sitting in front of me. As a therapist, I realized I was the person sitting in the room experiencing the family, and that is powerful and important. My felt sense as a therapist should not be overlooked, and I could take my felt sense to supervision instead of relinquishing my experience to my supervisor. I realized I could speak more freely in supervision and assert information to further the supervision process, instead of assuming my supervisor's experience trumped my own. I learned to start trusting myself.

As a therapist who continues to be emotionally focused, I learned from this case and others to not fear my own vulnerability. Emotion-focused work is not for the faint of heart. I cried in supervision, to my husband, during case presentations, and even writing this chapter. I am stronger because of it. My supervisor helped me to accept my own humanity as a therapist. She would say things like, "So what if I cry? I'm human!" She was right. She would also say, "You are not your emotions." I have heard her say that repeatedly and I needed to hear it most of the times she said it. I am not my son's pain. When we talk about the pain in our family now, it is *less* powerful, not more. I know that now.

Part III Conclusion

The importance of self-of-the-therapist work in learning to be a therapist cannot be overstated. The therapists in these preceding chapters bravely describe their own process of reflecting on hidden agendas, secret fears, and mirrored imitations. Each of them shares a process of embracing vulnerability and utilizing transparency with their clients. Further, as truly experiential therapists, they engage their supervisor in making the covert, overt (Connell, Mitten, & Bumberry, 1999; Pickover, 2017). They approach their self-of-the-therapist reactions to better explore their personal experiences and the impact they have on their conceptualizations of clients and clinical interventions. As Satir (2000) emphasizes, "While therapists facilitate and enhance patients' ability and need to grow, they should at the same time be aware that they have the same ability and need" (p. 21). This growth process is required for in-session authenticity. Therapists' vulnerability, and their self-of-the-therapist work outside of session, promotes honesty and congruence, such that patients, themselves, can be more vulnerable.

While this process of growth in order to better use the self as an instrument of healing is done individually, in part, supervision is a key piece of highlighting and drawing out client–therapist overlaps that may be outside the therapist's awareness. However, as the supervisor introductions to each of these chapters highlight, supervisors are also vulnerable and regularly question their process of teaching and guiding trainees. Supervisors have an eye on multiple boundaries – between a therapist's family-of-origin and client families; between historical experiences and the here and now; between what happens in session and what gets communicated by clients to invested referrers; between supervisor and supervisee. Thus, clients, therapists, and supervisors all ask, *Am I enough?* A crisis of confidence is not a death knell. It is likely, paradoxically, both a developmentally appropriate stage for the new therapist, as well as a sign of maturity. Using this reaction isomorphically, to inform where in the system it may be most meaningful to intervene, can be an especially powerful intervention based on the therapist's use of self.

Thought Questions

1. Are you aware when a client's family reflects your own family? When this happens, do you ask for help from your supervisor? Or do you have trouble asking for help, out of fear of embarrassment or appearing incompetent?

2. If you (or a colleague) have ever struggled to ask a supervisor for help with self-of-the-therapist issues, how might that reflect clients' struggles to be vulnerable? How might avoiding asking for help in supervision impact the progress of therapy?

3. Can you identify strengths of your own family-of-origin that may benefit/have benefited you as a therapist?

4. What are the boundaries between self-of-the-therapist work in supervision and personal therapy? How would you describe the difference? Would you wait for a supervisor to identify you're approaching this boundary?

5. How would you react if a supervisor suggested you seek personal therapy?

6. What is the difference between transparency in therapy and self-disclosure? When could self-disclosure with clients be problematic? If you decided to self-disclose, how could you ensure it is therapeutic and for the clients' benefit?

7. When the therapy goal changes, how flexible are you in adjusting to the change? Do you feel you have failed if the original goal is not met?

8. Do you ever feel you are more attached to the goal, or more tied to the results, than your clients? Authors in this part as well as in Part II, use the term "divine detachment" – how would you describe this?

9. Are you able to let go of your cases upon completion or does a case linger on long after you have terminated? What contributes to the difference?

Part IV

CONCLUDING REMARKS ON SUPERVISION

Trusted supervisor colleagues are essential. It is vital for supervisors to debrief with trusted colleagues in order to discuss difficult cases and check on whether one is truly being helpful to a trainee. When a supervisor is too close to the work, it is critical to get another's perspective in order to gain clarity. This aligns with what we expect of supervisees – that they will come to us and confer when they're struggling to see the full picture. This process of consultation and debriefing allows us to have trust across the therapeutic system.

Struggle is (mostly) normal. The central purpose of this book is to comfort and encourage couple and family therapists beginning their careers by normalizing that learning the work can be a struggle. These therapist authors struggled, it's ok to struggle, and it's normal to have doubts and fears and wonder if you're in the right business.

However, there's a difference between observing and teaching around that struggle, as a supervisor, when a trainee's struggle may really mean they cannot do the work. When you become a supervisor, you are making a commitment to the profession in overseeing that quality therapists enter the field. The responsibility of teasing out normative challenges from rare indicators of a professional lack of fit lies with the supervisor. Nonmalefi- cence is a critical ethical principle to uphold, in that clients' well-being must always be a supervisor's consideration. It is not easy to have gate- keeping conversations. Thus, this is another area where consulting with a supervisor peer is essential. Gatekeeping can feel like trammeling a learner's dreams, yet the trainees we supervise will reflect on the profession as a whole.

Launching is hard. It is always bittersweet when you realize that the intern you have supervised for years is now ready to move on. The first sign comes when a trainee needs little guidance and can speak about their cases from a sense of knowing what to do and how the case needs to progress. You find yourself enjoying their successes and admiring their work. The supervisory relationship develops and transitions; super- vision turns into mentoring with discussions about the business of therapy, networking, promoting oneself in the private sector, or launch- ing into new work settings. The supervisor becomes a bystander, watch- ing the intern take on a professional mantle. Supervisors then get to experience a sense of accomplishment: you have done your best and have helped to evolve a new trusted colleague. You can then hold hope that what you have passed on will be passed forward.

REFERENCES

American Association of Marriage and Family Therapy. (2018). *Competencies for family therapists working in healthcare settings*. Retrieved from www.aamft.org/healthcare

Anderson, S. A., Schlossberg, M., & Rigazio-DiGilio, S. (2000). Family therapy trainees' evaluations of their best and worst supervision experiences. *Journal of Marital and Family Therapy, 26*(1), 79–91. doi: 10.1111/j.1752-0606.2000.tb00278.x

Aponte, H. J. (1982). The cornerstone of therapy: The person of the therapist. *The Family Therapy Networker, 6*, 19–21.

Aponte, H. J. (2016). The person-of-the-therapist model on the use of self in therapy: The training philosophy. In H. J. Aponte & K. Kissil (Eds.), *The person of the therapist training model: Mastering the use of self* (pp. 1–13). New York: Routledge.

Aponte, H. J., & Kissil, K. (2014). If I can grapple with this, I can truly be of use in the therapy room: Using the therapist's own emotional struggles to facilitate effective therapy. *Journal of Marital and Family Therapy, 40*(2), 152–164. doi: 10.1111/jmft.12011

Aponte, H. J., & Winter, J. E. (2000). The person and practice of the therapist: Treatment and training. In M. Baldwin (Ed.), *The use of self in therapy* (2nd ed., pp. 127–165). BinghBinghamton, NY: The Haworth Press.

Bischoff, R. J., Barton, M., Thober, J., & Hawley, R. (2002). Events and experiences impacting the development of clinical self confidence: A study of the first year of client contact. *Journal of Marital and Family Therapy, 28*(3), 371–382. doi: 10.1111/j.1752-0606.2002.tb01193.x

Blow, A. J., & Sprenkle, D. H. (2001). Common factors across theories of marriage and family therapy: A modified Delphi study. *Journal of Marital and Family Therapy, 27*, 385–401. doi: 10.1111/j.1752-0606.2001.tb00333.x

Bok, S. (1982). *Secrets: On the ethics of concealment & revelations.* New York: Pantheon Books.

Boszormenyi-Nagy, I., & Krasner, B. R. (1986). *Between give & take: A clinical guide to contextual therapy.* New York: Brunner-Routledge.

Braverman, S. (1997). The use of genograms in supervision. In T. Todd & C. Storm (Eds.), *The complete systemic supervisor: Context, philosophy, and pragmatics* (pp. 156–172). Boston, MA: Allyn and Bacon.

Brown, J. (1999). Bowen family systems theory and practice: Illustration and critique. *Australian & New Zealand Journal of Family Therapy, 20*(2), 94–103. doi:10.1002/j.1467-8438.1999.tb00363.x

Byock, I. (1997). *Dying well.* New York: Riverhead.

Connell, G. M., Mitten, T., & Bumberry, W. (1999). *Reshaping family relationships: The symbolic therapy of Carl Whitaker.* Philadelphia, PA: Brunner/Mazel.

Connell, G. M., Mitten, T. J., & Whitaker, C. A. (1993). Reshaping family symbols: A symbolic-experiential perspective. *Journal of Marital and Family Therapy, 19*(3), 243–251. doi: 10.1111/j.1752-0606.1993.tb00985.x

D'Arrigo-Patrick, J., Hoff, C., Knudson-Martin, C., & Tuttle, A. (2017). Navigating critical theory and postmodernism: Social justice and therapist power in family therapy. *Family Process, 56*, 574–588. doi:10.1111/famp.12236

Engel, G. L. (1977). The need for a new medical model: A challenge for biomedicine. *Science, 196*, 129–136. doi:10.1126/science.847460

Engel, G. L. (1980). The clinical application of the biopsychosocial model. *The American Journal of Psychiatry, 137*, 535–544. doi:10.1176/ajp.137.5.535

Frediani, G., & Rober, P. (2016). What novice family therapists experience during a session … A qualitative study of novice therapists' inner conversations during the session. *Journal of Marital and Family Therapy, 42*(3), 481–494. doi:10.1111/jmft.12149

Freedman, J., & Combs, G. (1996). *Narrative therapy: The social construction of preferred realities.* New York: W. W. Norton & Company.

Grolnick, L. (1983). Ibsen's truth, family secrets, and family therapy. *Family Process, 22*, 275–288. doi: 10.1111/j.1545-5300.1983.00275.x

Imber-Black, E. (1998). *The secret life of families. Making decisions about secrets: When keeping secrets can harm you, when keeping secrets can heal you- and how to know the difference.* New York: Bantam Books.

Johnson, S. (2005). *Becoming an emotionally focused couple therapist: The workbook.* New York: Routledge.

Karpel, M. A. (1980). Family secrets: I. Conceptual and ethical issues in the relational context. II. Ethical and practical considerations in therapeutic management. *Family Process, 19*(3), 295–306. doi: 10.1111/j.1545-5300.1980.00295.x

Keith, D. (2000). The self in family therapy: A field guide. In M. Baldwin (Ed.), *The use of self in therapy* (2nd ed., pp. 263–274). Binghamton, NY: The Haworth Press.

Kerr, M. E., & Bowen, M. (1988). *Family evaluation: An approach based on Bowen theory.* New York: W. W. Norton & Company.

Knudson-Martin, C. (1994). The female voice: Applications to Bowen's family systems theory. *Journal of Marital and Family Therapy, 20*(1), 35–46. doi: 10.1111/j.1752-0606.1994.tb01009.x

Knudson-Martin, C. (2013). Why power matters: Creating a foundation of mutual support in couple relationships. *Family Process, 52*(1), 5–18. doi:10.1111/famp.12011

Liddle, H. A., & Saba, G. W. (1983). On context replication: The isomoprhic relationship of training and therapy. *Journal of Strategic and Systemic Therapies*, 2, 3–11. doi: 10.1521/jsst.1983.2.2.3

Linehan, M. M. (2015). *DBT® skills training manual* (2nd ed.). New York: The Guilford Press.

Lum, W. (2002). The use of self of the therapist. *Contemporary Family Therapy*, 24(1), 181–197. doi: 10.1023/A:1014385908625

May, G. (1982). *Will and spirit.* San Francisco, CA: Harper & Row.

McDaniel, S. H., Doherty, W. J., & Hepworth, J. (2014). *Medical family therapy and integrated care* (2nd ed.). Washington, DC: American Psychological Association.

McDowell, T., Knudson-Martin, C., & Bermudez, J. M. (2018). *Socioculturally attuned family therapy: Guidelines for equitable theory and practice.* New York: Routledge/Taylor & Francis. doi:10.1007/978-3-319-15877-8

McDowell, T., Knudson-Martin, C., & Bermudez, J. M. (2019). Third-order thinking in family therapy: Addressing social justice across family therapy practice. *Family Process*, 58(1), 9–22. doi: 10.1111/famp.12383

Minuchin, S., & Fishman, H. C. (1981). *Family therapy techniques.* Cambridge, MA: Harvard University Press.

Mitten, T. J., & Connell, G. M. (2004). The core variables of symbolic-experiential therapy: A qualitative study. *Journal of Marital and Family Therapy*, 30(4), 467–478. doi: 10.1111/j.1752-0606.2004.tb01256.x

Morgan, M. M., & Sprenkle, D. H. (2007). Toward a common-factors approach to supervision. *Journal of Marital and Family Therapy*, 33(1), 1–17. doi: 10.1111/j.1752-0606.2007.00001.x

Patterson, J., Williams, L., Edwards, T. M., Chamow, L., & Grauf-Grounds, C. (2018). *Essential skills in family therapy: From the first interview to termination.* New York: The Guilford Press.

Peek, C. J. (2008). Planning care in the clinical, operational, and financial worlds. In R. Kessler & D. Stafford (Eds.), *Collaborative medicine case studies* (pp. 25–38). New York: Springer. doi:10.1007/978-0-387-76894-6_3

Pickover, S. (2017). Metaphors. In J. Carlson & S. B. Dermer (Eds.), *The SAGE encyclopedia of marriage, family, and couples counseling* (Vol. 3, pp. 1063–1067). Thousand Oaks, CA: SAGE Publications, Inc. doi:10.4135/9781483369532.n319

Rønnestad, M. H., & Skovholt, T. M. (2003). The journey of the counselor and therapist: Research findings and perspectives on professional development. *Journal of Career Development*, 30(1), 5–44. doi: 10.1023/A:1025173508081

Satir, V. (2000). The therapist story. In M. Baldwin (Ed.), *The use of self in therapy* (2nd ed., pp. 1717–1727). Binghamton, NY: The Haworth Press.

Satir, V., & Baldwin, M. (1983). *Satir step by step: A guide to creating change in families.* Palo Alto, CA: Science & Behavior Books.

Satir, V., Banmen, J., Gerber, J., & Gomori, M. (1991). *The Satir model: Family therapy and beyond.* Palo Alto, CA: Science & Behavior Books.

Shellenberger, S., Dent, M. M., Davis-Smith, M., Seale, J. P., Weintraut, R., & Wright, T. (2007). Cultural genogram: A tool for teaching and practice. *Families, Systems, & Health*, 25(4), 367–381. doi:10.1037/1091-7527.25.4.367

Simon, G. M. (2006). The heart of the matter: A proposal for placing the self of the therapist at the center of family therapy research and training. *Family Process*, 45, 331–344. doi: 10.1111/j.1545-5300.2006.00174.x

Sprenkle, D. H., & Blow, A. J. (2004). Common factors and our sacred models. *Journal of Marital and Family Therapy, 30*(2), 113–129. doi: 10.1111/j.1752-0606.2004.tb01228.x

Timm, T. M., & Blow, A. J. (1999). Self-of-the-therapist work: A balance between removing restraints and identifying resources. *Contemporary Family Therapy, 21*(3), 331–351. doi: 10.1023/A:1021960315503

Tolle, E. (2005). *A new earth: Awakening to your life's purpose.* New York: Penguin Group.

von Bertalanffy, L. (1968). *General systems theory: Foundations, development, applications.* New York: George Braziller.

Weir, K. N. (2009). Countering the isomorphic study of isomorphism: Coercive, mimetic, and normative isomorphic trends in the training, supervision, and industry of marriage and family therapy. *Journal of Family Psychotherapy, 20*(1), 60–61. doi:10.1080/08975350802716517

Whitaker, C. A. (1973). My philosophy of psychotherapy. *Journal of Contemporary Psychotherapy, 6,* 49–52. doi: 10.1007/BF01796033

Whitaker, C. (1989). *Midnight musings of a family therapist.* M. O. Ryan (Ed.). New York: W. W. Norton & Company.

Whitaker, C. A., & Malone, T. P. (1953). *The roots of psychotherapy.* New York: Blakiston.

White, M., & Epston, D. (1990). *Narrative means to therapeutic ends.* New York: W. W. Norton & Company.

White, M., & Russell, C. S. (1997). Examining the multifaceted notion of isomorphism in marriage and family therapy supervision: A quest for conceptual clarity. *Journal of Marital and Family Therapy, 23*(3), 315–333. doi: 10.1111/j.1752-0606.1997.tb01040.x

INDEX

addiction 62, 69, 97

advocacy ethics 45

amyotrophic lateral sclerosis 15, 72

anticipatory grief 96, 98

anxiety 6, 7, 18, 28, 33, 38, 45, 53,
64, 69, 71, 73, 81–85, 100–102,
105, 107, 111, 115

attachment 18, 94; wounds 68,
89, 93

Attention-Deficit/Hyperactivity
Disorder 52

autism 118, 120, 122, 125

autonomy 4, 7, 81, 85, 86

behavioral management 54, 55

biopsychosocial 27, 43

boundaries 6–7, 24, 40, 43, 57, 85,
124, 128, 129

Bowen, M. 3, 6–7, 63, 82; Bowenian
interventions 81

catching the disease 47

child protective services (CPS) 51,
56, 57

children's hospital 50–52,
55, 117

Christian counseling 102

circular pattern 18

circular questioning 45

collaboration 2, 3, 13, 43–44, 47, 49,
73, 75, 88

competence 23, 40, 75, 79, 83, 85,
87, 92, 94, 100; incompetence 4,
84, 91–92, 94

connection 2, 8–10, 17–19, 21–23,
44, 49, 52, 60–61, 70–71, 74, 81,
84, 101; disconnection 7, 18, 70;
interconnection 43

contextual family therapy 8

couple therapy 15, 18, 25, 28, 80,
89–90, 93, 116

couple's cycle 30, 34–36
cycle of chaos 56

de-escalate 69, 90
depressive symptoms 110
destructive entitlement 8
detached 114
diagnosis 64, 67, 69, 70, 72, 95,
    116–119, 120, 126
differentiation 6, 81
disease 25, 47–48, 61, 64, 75,
    114, 116
disengaged families 7, 8
divine detachment 59, 114, 129
dysfunctional 68

Emotionally Focused Couple Therapy
    15, 18, 25, 80, 90, 116
empower 43; disempower 74,
    83, 114
equifinality 47
experiential model 82

family of origin 3, 9, 13, 28, 40, 65,
    81–82, 95–96, 103, 114–115, 120,
    128–129
family therapy 2–9, 15, 41–45,
    47, 50–52, 56, 67, 73–74,
    80–82, 84, 88–90, 96, 101,
    103, 113–114, 116

general systems theory 43
genetic counselor 117
genogram 44, 66–67, 95, 98, 115
grief 13, 15–17, 19, 20–21,
    23, 26, 31, 38, 64, 96, 98,
    99, 110

healthcare 43–44, 62–63, 68, 74
hopeless 48, 119
humanistic experiential approach 83
hypothesis 96

imposter syndrome 84
interaction cycle 118
interdisciplinary 62; team 63
interface 24
interventions 70; clinical 128;
    supervisory 3, 44, 47–48;
    therapeutic 46
isomorph 3, 9–11, 14, 23, 40, 77, 85,
    100, 128

Klippel Feil Syndrome (KFS) 116,
    122, 126

larger systems 3, 41–45, 47, 49–50,
    75, 114

macrosystem 41
medical family therapy 3, 42–43, 88

narrative therapy 42
negative cycle 19

one-down position 65, 99
Oppositional Defiant Disorder 52

palliative care 96
paradigms 47–48
paradox 119; paradoxical 101;
    paradoxically 128
patient-centered 62–63
patterns 3, 6, 9–10, 35, 64, 68, 77,
    80, 114

person of the therapist 4, 79, 91
person-of-the-therapist model (POTT) 80, 82
poetry 72
Post-Traumatic Stress Disorder 52
power dynamics 46–47, 83
powerless 53, 76, 121; powerlessness 59, 122
psych ER 60, 62–64, 66, 68, 70, 72
psychiatrist 15, 66–69
pursue-withdraw pattern 18

rare metabolic disorder 118
reframe 60, 76, 97, 118, 122, 126
role-play 34, 47

schizophrenia 62, 70
second career 31, 48, 75
secrets 3, 5, 6–11, 24, 26, 29–31, 34–36, 39–40
self-disclosure 27, 105, 129
self-esteem 79
self-of-the-therapist 2–3, 9, 13, 16, 24, 29, 31, 38–39, 77–79, 81, 83–86, 108, 111, 113, 115, 128–129
sexual orientation 31–32, 35, 103
sexual trauma 33–34
shame 28, 30–31, 33–35, 37, 91, 92, 104
signature themes 80
social justice 45–46
social worker 56, 62–68, 73

special needs 121, 122
spiritual 26, 28–30, 61
split loyalties 8
strengths 14, 24, 27, 30; strength-based 13, 46, 63, 67, 77–79, 82, 85, 112, 129
struggle(s) 2, 26, 46–47, 55, 61, 100–109, 113–115, 122, 126, 129, 131; struggled 51, 54–55, 58, 94, 104, 109, 115, 126, 129, 131
subsystems 3, 39, 54, 66
suicide 13, 20, 73, 103, 104
symbolic experiential 82

therapeutic touch 62, 71
third-order change/thinking 46
transgender 101–103, 108, 110
trauma(s) 3, 5, 9–10, 13–14, 25, 30–36, 40, 71–72, 78, 89, 116
triangles 6, 45

unanticipated disclosure 6
universal healing 71

validation 16–17, 25, 51, 56, 58, 61, 98, 121–122, 125
Vegas rule 78
vulnerability 2, 4, 20–23, 27–28, 33, 36–38, 54, 59, 83, 87, 89, 92–93, 107, 110–111, 128–129

whole system 60, 118
workability 121

Made in United States
North Haven, CT
25 August 2022

23243700R00087